Pulled Thread Embroidery

Stitches, techniques and over 140 exquisite designs

SEARCH PRESS

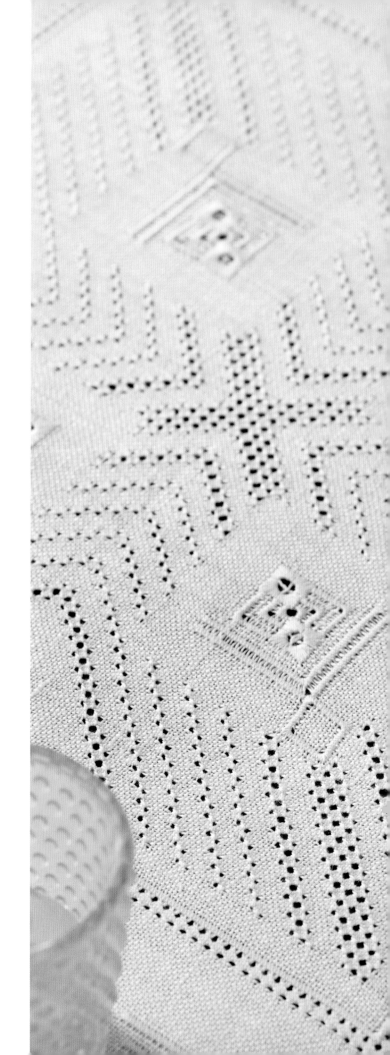

First published in Great Britain 2021 by
Search Press Limited
Wellwood
North Farm Road
Tunbridge Wells
Kent TN2 3DR

First published in French by Éditions Un Dimanche Après Midi,
France as *Jours à fils reserrés - technique d'une broderie ajourée sans fils
coupés ni fils tirés*

© 2019 by Éditions Un Dimanche Après Midi/Huapango

English translation by Burravoe Translation Services

Editor: Alexis Faja
Photo styling: Charlotte Vannier
Photos: Didier Bizet/portait (p. 143): Etienne Audebrand

ISBN: 978-1-78221-843-2

If you have difficulty in obtaining any of the materials and equipment
mentioned in this book, then please visit the Search Press website for
details of suppliers: www.searchpress.com

Contents

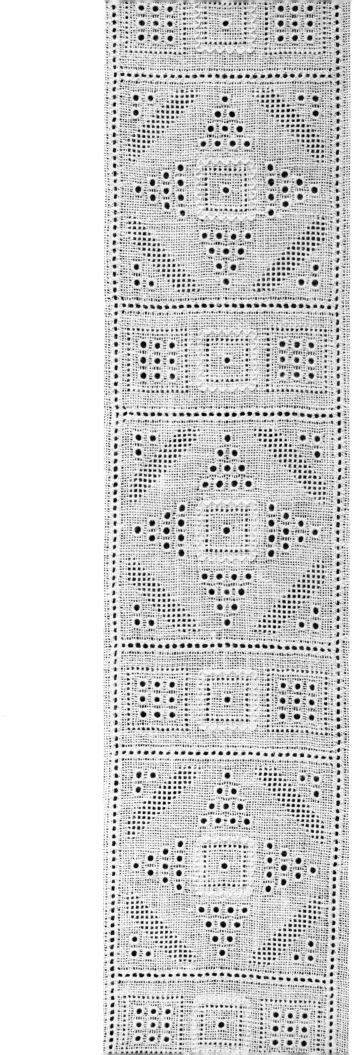

PULLED THREAD EMBROIDERY

- What is it? -

Also known as 'counted thread openwork', 'pulled thread work' or 'drawn thread work', this is an openwork effect achieved by simply using sewing thread to pull on the threads of the fabric, without cutting or removing them. It is worked on loosely woven fabrics, using a fine tapestry needle, and involves counting the threads. The effects vary depending on which stitches are used, how tightly or loosely the fabric is woven and the characteristics of the sewing thread. The result is an intricate, lace-like design.

The basic stitches can be combined into a multitude of decorative embroidery patterns creating elegant embellishment for numerous items such as table linen, curtains, lampshades and small personal accessories. Some of these stitches can be used to outline patterns and create openwork motifs, alone or in combination, while others are for filling in larger or smaller areas. Pulled thread work can be used on its own or combined with other techniques: embroidery, patchwork, French quilting... let your imagination run riot.

Although pulled thread embroidery has ancient origins, it is very suited to modern-day decorative use, and opens up infinite creative possibilities, both in terms of the patterns and the stitches themselves – you can easily create your own.

- Origins -

Counted thread openwork has been used in several regions of the world, often associated with satin stitch or other stitches, giving rise to a wide variety of embroidery styles. It is found on 19th century embroidery from Iran, in the traditional costume of several regions of the Ukraine, in France on the traditional headdresses of Normandy and other regions (more specifically the 'Pèleboise' headdresses of Deux-Sèvres), in certain Chikankari embroideries in India, as well as in many other countries. It often forms geometric patterns (Iran, Ukraine, Pèleboise headdresses), or sometimes takes a much freer form (India).

However, these techniques enjoyed particular popularity in 18th century Europe, especially in the Dresden region of Germany, where incredible whitework was produced on sheer, fine cambrics. We also still have some similar pieces of the same era from Denmark, England and Switzerland, so it seems that much of Anglo-Saxon Europe produced or used it. These fine fabrics were generally decorated with floral motifs: each part of the motif was filled with openwork or satin stitches and then outlined in a heavier stitch; sometimes the background was also openwork. Many items were embroidered in this way, including bonnets, scarves, aprons, cuffs and even waistcoats, which were then quilted. The talent and imagination of the embroiderers of that era is breathtaking, as is the diversity of embroidery designs used.

Schwalm embroidery, where the openwork background is worked in drawn or pulled threads depending on the fabric used, is sometimes considered to be a popular version of Dresden embroidery. Its designs of birds, hearts and tulips are characteristic of this style of embroidery and the majority of the openwork shown here may be used for it.

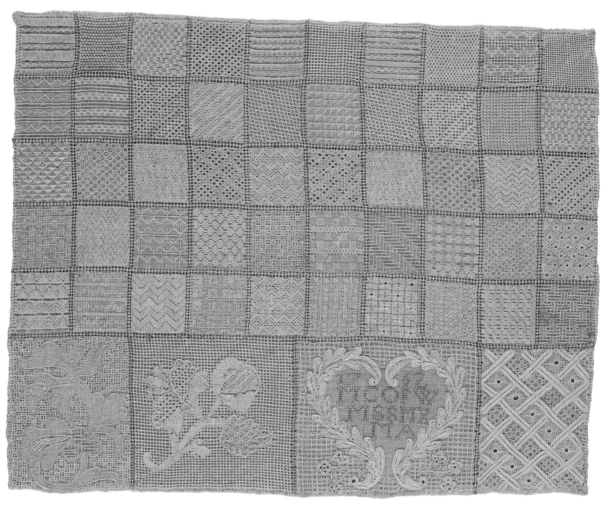

German sampler 1762,
© Museum of Fine Arts, Boston

- How it is used -

As mentioned previously, traditional embroideries generally take one of two forms:

- geometric compositions, where pulled stitches form lines which are generally straight, or areas of openwork that are themselves geometric. Openwork stitches may be accompanied by other stitches, most often straight stitches as in embroidery on fabric, but also some traditional embroidery stitches. The composition often emerges from the pulled thread stitches themselves, combined freely with other stitches and only bordered by the fabric that is left unpulled around them. Sometimes straight stitches or other stitches outline the areas of openwork, which then form part of a larger composition.

- free (or traced) designs formed of patterns of flowers, birds, hearts, and so on. The motifs are outlined by stitches worked with a heavier thread such as chain, coral or scallop stitch. The inside of these motifs and even the background in some embroidered lace, is filled with drawn thread work, sometimes combined with satin stitches.

While by nature the geometric compositions are perhaps more contemporary, both types of composition can be tailored to today's tastes. A simple combination of stitch samples can in itself create a lovely effect, as in the example shown above.

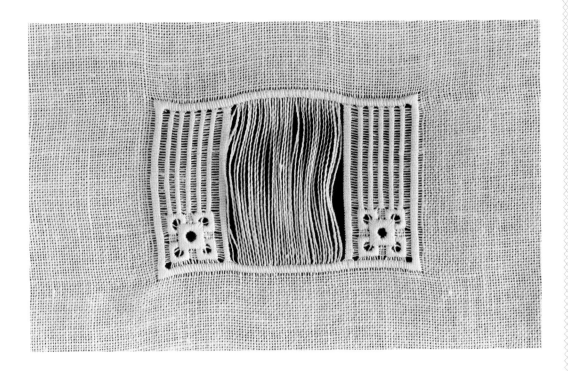

The most important thing is to give it a go; there are infinite sources of inspiration to be found – look at the patterns used for other embroidery techniques or take inspiration from art, crafts or the world around you.

- Self-coloured or contrasted? -

One question I am often asked is about the use of colour. Pulled thread embroidery is generally worked white on white, or at least self-coloured, and this is indeed how it looks its best, as the interest of openwork lies in the contrast of empty and filled areas, holes and transparencies.

However, there is nothing to stop you embroidering on coloured fabric with matching threads, or using an embroidery thread that is a slightly different shade from the background colour: a pearl grey on white for example, or ecru on a natural linen background. On the other hand, the use of contrasting colour would reduce the impact, highlighting the thread stitches, which are not of any particular interest in themselves. There is one exception, however: when only one stitch is used in a composition, and this stitch provides fairly wide coverage, colour can be used to provide variation or, as in the sample opposite, it can be used to add definition.

MATERIALS AND ACCESSORIES

- Fabric -

Pulled thread embroidery is usually worked on an evenweave fabric; it must be sufficiently loosely woven to enable you to pull the threads without difficulty as you embroider, thus obtaining the attractive openwork effect. On a more tightly woven fabric, the stitches will tend to create texture without really creating holes in the fabric, and can cause it to pucker if the weave is very tight. In addition, to achieve horizontal and vertical symmetry, the fabric must be balanced, that is, it must have the same number of threads of the same thickness, in both the weft and the warp. This is very important for numerous patterns and for all square items or items that feature designs with a square symmetry.

Linen evenweaves are nice to work with and give an excellent result. They drape beautifully and the slight irregularity of the weave gives them a more interesting finish. They come in different thicknesses, around 18 threads per inch for the loosest weave in comparison with 55 or indeed 60 threads per inch for cambrics, for example. Choose your fabric on the basis of the result you want, the purpose of your project, your skill level and your eyesight! Linen voile is more delicate to use but can provide some very interesting effects, given that the majority of voiles are not balanced in terms of warp and weft count.

Cotton evenweaves are often more tightly woven and less easy to handle, unless you opt for cheesecloth, which is cheap and gives a great finish if the weave is sufficiently regular.

Synthetic evenweaves (such as modal) can be very regular or, by contrast, manufactured using more irregular threads to resemble a linen evenweave. I find them less satisfying to handle, but it is worth giving them a try as they look good and work perfectly for some uses.

You could also try experimenting with wool or silk evenweaves for items such as sophisticated scarves and stoles. Note, however, that they are not always balanced in terms of warp and weft threads! Silk gauze is not suitable; it has a more complex, rigid weave that makes it almost impossible to displace the threads.

- Thread -

The thread used must be fine but strong enough to withstand the tension of the significant strain of repeated pulling and to ensure it will not fluff when passing through the fabric. By way of example, to maintain the lace effect, the thickest thread to use for a 25-count fabric would be a size 12 pearl cotton or DMC cordonnet no. 50. Remember that for the same quality of thread, the higher the number, the finer the thread (i.e. 100 is finer than 50). Stranded threads, whether cotton, silk, linen or rayon, must only be used for satin stitches. They are too fragile for pulled stitches (with the odd exception, such as using short lengths of thread on a very supple fabric).

Lace threads have a crisper, more solid finish, and come in several thicknesses. DMC cordonnet (Cordonnet Spécial) ranges from no. 10 to no. 100 in white and ecru. DMC has a lace thread, dentelle no. 80 (Special Dentelles 80) in around 30 colours and you will find other brands with different colours at your local sewing shop (Venus, Cocon Calais, and so on) or online.

DMC coton à broder (Special Embroidery Thread), used generally for whitework, is rounder and gives more texture. It comes in four thicknesses in white and ecru (16, 20, 25 and 30) and 173 colours in no. 25. It gives a little more body and texture to the embroidery and works very well for certain pulled thread work projects.

DMC's hand and machine quilting thread, for thick fabric, is supple and tightly wound and is another excellent choice for anything that requires a fine thread.

Other, waxed, quilting threads are too stiff to use satisfactorily. Oliver Twists' mercerized cotton thread is nicely solid and supple and offers some very subtle shades to work with on colour. Egyptian cotton by the brand Au Chinois is likewise very solid. Here again, there are numerous brands to try as soon as you have confidence in your abilities: however, on a linen or cotton closeweave fabric, avoid the majority of synthetic threads, which will not take well to being ironed.

Aurifil thread comes in three thicknesses and 216 colours. It is very supple and quite solid, and has more of a shine than the others mentioned above. Depending on which stitches you use, the Maestoso (a more flexible version of pearl no. 12) and Vivace ranges can do a great job. Allegro, the finest, is more fragile and is only really suitable for finer, lighter fabrics.

Metallic threads are often too fragile for thread-counted openwork and do not take well to repeated washing or hot ironing: as a result they should only be used for decorative work, to add a little shimmer to festive embroideries.

Silk threads look great and give a very sophisticated finish. However, as with other threads, they must be sufficiently robust to withstand the tension of pulling the threads of the fabric: the pearl silk (365 colours) and silk 1003 (780 colours) by Au Ver à Soie are very nice to work with and give a great finish.

Linen threads for lace are not really supple enough, but are sufficiently solid and can be of interest for a more matte, natural finish. They come in several thicknesses and colours.

- Tools -

Needles

Blunt tapestry needles are best so as not to snag the threads of the fabric. The size you choose will depend on the thickness of your fabric and your personal preferences. I normally use size 24 or size 26 for day-to-day fabrics; size 28 for finer ones.

To work in the ends of the embroidery threads under the stitches you have already sewn so they cannot be seen, it is best to change needle and use a fine sewing needle of the right size for the thickness of thread you are using.

Embroidery hoop or frame

Working with the fabric stretched over an embroidery frame or hoop will help you achieve a more regular finish. When stitching an outline, it is possible to do without a frame as long as you can manage to stretch your fabric as you work, and it is sometimes more practical for borders. However, a frame or hoop is essential when filling and you can work with the fabric at a looser tension if you prefer forming the stitch in one movement. If you use a hoop with legs or on a stand, both hands are free and you can work with one above and one below the fabric, pulling your thread firmly when it is underneath.

When I take beginners' workshops I often use plastic or metal hoops, which are practical as they are quick to set up and pack away. As these hoops are designed for machine embroidery, I don't use them for the work that I do by hand, and I don't recommend them for general use as they can snag fabric, displacing the threads of the fabric and crushing the embroidery that you have already done. I would opt for wooden frames. They take a little longer to set up, but they work better with your embroidery: if you wrap a strip of fabric round each ring of the hoop (strips from an old sheet will do the trick), you will achieve a firm but flexible tension without damaging your fabric or embroidery.

For samples and small and medium-sized pieces, working on a frame can be a comfortable option; there are frames of all sizes and to suit all budgets that are easy to transport.

Scissors and thimbles

You will need sewing scissors for your fabric and your usual embroidery scissors for your thread. It is essential that both are nice and sharp.

A thimble will protect your fingers if you are embroidering for long periods and is essential for pushing the needle when you are working in the tails of thread at the end.

GETTING STARTED

- The best options -

I would recommend starting with a white or ecru linen evenweave fabric of average thickness: 25 to 38 count, for example. This is pleasant to work with and will not tire your eyes. When you have mastered the basic stitches and the 'right' tension for this fabric, you can use finer or thicker fabric depending on the type of thread used.

For fabric with a 25 to 30 thread count, start with a fine thread for most of the stitches, for example DMC dentelle no. 80 or DMC cordonnet no. 100 thread or Aurifil Vivace thread. Some stitches require a thread that is a little less fine: I will highlight them in the relevant chapter. When you have got the hang of a stitch, play around with different thicknesses and qualities of thread: you will soon find your favourite threads and learn to use them to achieve the effect you want.

- Before you begin -

Start by oversewing all round the edges of your fabric to ensure it does not fray while you are working – this can happen very easily with loosely woven fabrics.

For a symmetrical composition, you will then need to put in some markers: fold your fabric in four to find the middle, then mark it with a small cross made with a coloured tacking thread. If you are working on a larger project, work a backstitch with this same thread every 50 threads of the fabric: this is a bit fiddly but will save you lots of time at a later stage and is a good way of avoiding subsequent mistakes. If needed, you could also tack along the main lines of your composition. If marking the mid-point is sufficient, work a long backstitch in coloured thread and then add any extra marks you need to facilitate your embroidery.

If your composition is geometric, you can start your embroidery as soon as you have put in your markers: these will act as a guide whether the design is a product of your imagination or taken from a pattern.

If you are embroidering a design from a pattern, transfer the pattern to your fabric before you begin. There are several ways of doing this:

- use an iron-on pattern;
- trace the pattern onto tracing paper or silk paper and then copy it onto the fabric using carbon paper; carbon paper comes in several colours, so choose one that will show up against your background;
- if your fabric is fairly transparent, place the pattern underneath and trace directly onto your fabric with a special water-based fabric marker; it is often the best method for the fabrics we will be using here, and the simplest as well;
- the traditional method, if you can get to grips with it, is as follows: trace your pattern onto some thin tracing paper; prick this tracing paper from the wrong side; place it on your fabric, weighing it down to hold it in place; then sprinkle it with pumice-stone powder to transfer your design, before fixing it with alcohol or an iron.

- Starting and finishing -

It is now time to thread your needle and get started! Two little tips:

- make sure your lengths of thread aren't too long – long thread may seem time saving but your back and shoulders will suffer;
- and in particular – a general rule in embroidery but most particularly in this case – never tie a knot in your thread.

Start your embroidery leaving a sufficient tail of thread for you to be able to work it subsequently into the first stitches or under the stitches outlining the pattern if relevant, always on the reverse of the work. When you need to work in your thread in the middle of a pattern or a line, make sure that you form the stitch as it would be formed in the course of the embroidery: stitches are pulled and tightened in a particular direction that you must respect when weaving the end of your thread under the stitches on the wrong side.

More often than not, you will have to leave the tail of your thread until later when you can work it under the stitches that you will work subsequently, and it will be the new thread that you can work under the stitches you have already made. However, this is not always the case: check which way your stitches are going in order to work out how best to make the change of thread invisible.

When you are working a filling inside a stitched outline, make sure that you start and finish under the outline: it is easier to work the tails of thread under this denser embroidery. In all cases, use as fine a sewing needle as possible and only work in the thread in one direction so the tails are hidden.

- Where to begin -

This is an important point when you are filling in a shape. In order to achieve a perfectly balanced pattern, you should start in the middle. Starting from this point, you will work half the row initially, leaving a sufficient length of thread to work the other half. For geometric patterns where the shape is not defined in advance, or if you are following a chart, the question does not arise in the same way: it is ease of counting that will determine the best starting point.

- Some tips -

The knot on the needle

As you need to pull quite hard to work the stitches, the thread has a tendency to slip out of the needle, which is very annoying. To avoid this, you need to tie a knot that will stop the thread coming out of the eye of the needle, as follows:

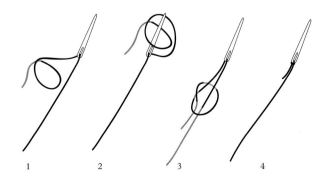

1   2   3   4

Moving from one row to the next without cutting the thread

Whichever stitch you are using, you should always work in the same direction. This means that you will never go 'out and back' on two adjacent rows, but rather you will rotate the work at the end of the row to work the next one. When transferring the thread from the end of one row to the beginning of the next you need to make sure that it does not show through the open area you have already formed. You may also find you need to bring the thread back up to start the new row in the same hole where you just finished. In such cases, you may need to form a small, discreet stitch or thread your way along the back of the fabric in order to bring it up in the right place. When two rows or two patterns are some distance away from each other, it is best to try to weave your thread as invisibly as possible through the threads of the fabric on the wrong side between the two: this is important both from an aesthetic point of view (the wrong side of your work will look much neater), and also from a practical point of view as it will prevent your iron from snagging on long threads and damaging your work when you are pressing it.

- Finishing -

There are several ways of finishing a piece. I will describe two here which, in my opinion, are the simplest and neatest:

* a classic hem with mitred corners, secured with hem stitch. This creates a very elegant finish and can also be highlighted by other pulled thread stitches, whatever your preference;
* on the majority of fabrics, you can trim the edges up to a row of pulled satin stitch, which gives you a wide range of possibilities when it comes to which stitches you use for the borders. This may not be possible on some very loosely woven fabrics, or ones where the threads slip easily; to be on the safe side, embroider several centimetres of pulled satin stitch and try to push the row obtained outwards: if it holds well you can use this type of finish without a problem; if it moves, you are better off with a hem.

Hem stitch (point de Paris)

* Fold the edges of your fabric under, wrong sides together (as in the diagram below), mark the corners with coloured thread (corner marker of your work) (b), then turn under again a few threads from the edge (c); press in these folds with an iron.
* Make your mitred corners: at each corner, fold your fabric right sides together on the diagonal (d) and sew at right angles to this fold from your corner marker (b), stopping when you reach the turned-under point of the hem (e). Cut off the excess fabric a few millimetres from the seam (f). Clip off the point at the top (g), flatten out the hem and turn your corner the right way out.

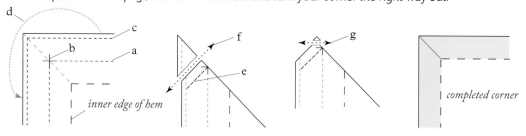

* Then sew your hem using hem stitch on the wrong side. Work from right to left:

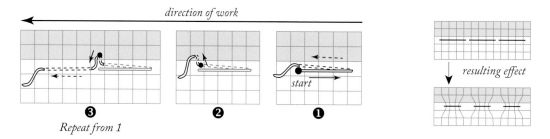

USING THIS BOOK

Following the essential information given in the first few pages of this book, which you can turn back to as a source of reference as you go, this book is organized into two parts:

- basic stitches, starting with the simplest and the most common: each is described with its advantages, its constraints and its uses. A detailed explanation is then given of the different ways the stitch can be worked. Details of possible variations are also given where relevant. For each one, including the variations, I make some suggestions for fillings that use the stitch, with a chart and photo of the stitched sample, and a 'how-to' diagram if necessary;
- fillings comprising combinations of stitches. There are an infinite number of combinations so this is not an exhaustive list, but rather an overview that gives some idea of the possibilities, providing you with tips that will allow you to progress and explore further avenues by yourself.

All the designs shown are taken from my book of samples. The majority are traditional designs found on works from the 18th century; some are personal creations, although it is impossible to say that no-one has done any given design before.

Unless indicated to the contrary, all these samples have been worked on Weddigen 26-count linen evenweave, using DMC threads. Details of the thread used is given for each sample.

Some diagrams have a red line to indicate the top of the work: it is useful as reference when you are rotating the work.

The instructions are given for right-handed people: I apologize to left-handed readers, who will need to work the mirror image.

Once you have got the hang of the technique, experiment with different threads and fabrics: the same pattern can give very different results depending on the materials you use.

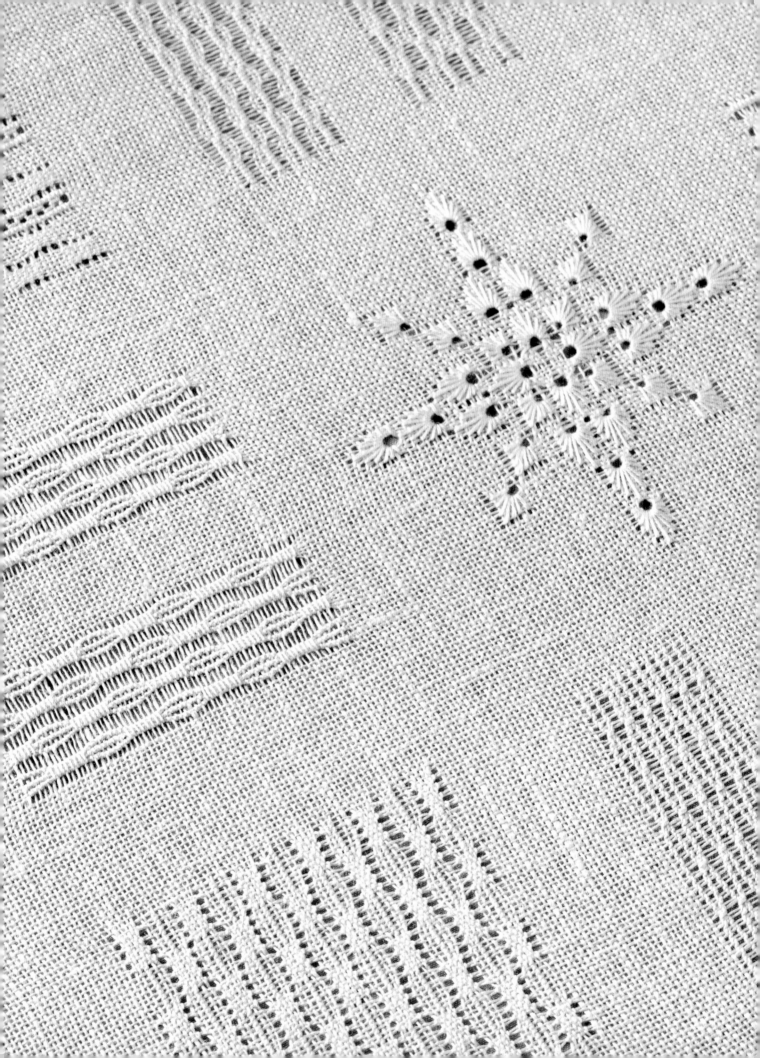

the basic stitches

SATIN STITCH

Whether in Dresden embroidery or the openwork embroidery of other regions of the world, satin stitch is used in two ways:

- in the usual way to create filled areas that complement the areas of pulled thread work and other textured stitches: these are the standard satin stitches used for surface embroidery;

- pulled tight to create a 'hole' in the fabric. In this case it is referred to as a 'pulled satin stitch'.

The basic movement is the same for both satin stitch and pulled satin stitch – it is the thread used and the tension applied that is different. The effect you achieve with satin stitches is exactly what you would expect it to be, since the threads of the fabric are not displaced. However, with pulled satin stitch, the effects vary depending on how it is used. For this reason, I will deal with them separately in more detail. The two options are represented differently in the diagrams: a thin line is used for the pulled satin stitches (and for other varieties of 'pulled' stitches), while a bolder line is used for the satin stitches.

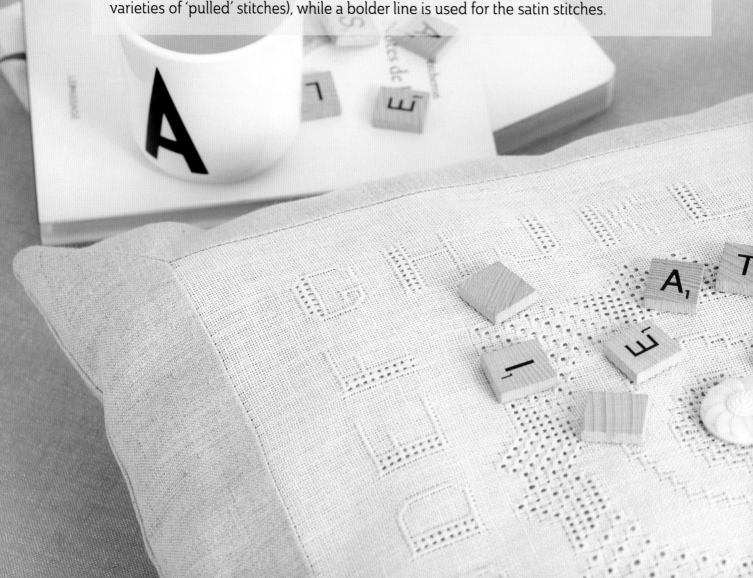

SATIN STITCH AND PULLED SATIN STITCH

Forming the stitch

- Satin stitch -

Satin stitches can be worked in line with the fabric weave or at an angle. They can be used to create a wide variety of patterns simply by varying stitch length or orientation. They can be used alone to give density against lacy areas of the pulled thread work that they border, or combined with pulled thread stitches in the same pattern to form a huge variety of fillings. Work from right to left, using a thread that is sufficiently thick for the fabric used: stranded embroidery floss, linen, silk or rayon thread, or any other that provides good coverage.

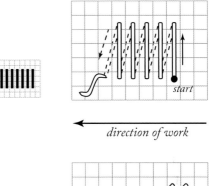

direction of work

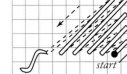

satin stitch
represented by bold lines on the diagrams

- Pulled satin stitch -

This is the simplest pulled thread stitch and also offers the widest range of possibilities; most openwork features it in some form or another. It creates nice clean lines which vary in height depending on whether you are working over 2, 3, 4, 5 or 6 threads of the fabric. You will generally wish to use a fine thread to achieve a lacy effect, but you may occasionally use a thicker thread to give a different finish, or emphasize a line or pattern.

Pulled satin stitch is worked between each thread of the background fabric: work from right to left as shown on the diagram, pulling firmly on the thread. To obtain regular holes of the same height all along the row, you must pull the thread perpendicularly to your fabric. If you want the hole created above the pulled threads to be larger than the one below, or vice versa, you will need to pull the thread flat against the fabric in the direction away from the hole that you want to be larger.

You can use this stitch on its own to create straight lines, to highlight patterns, to link them together, and so on. It is also useful for forming a wide variety of openwork fillings, on their own or in combination with other stitches. There is a great range of variations that can be used as the basic stitch for lines or blocks, on their own or in combination with other stitches.

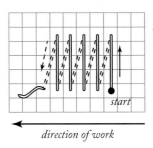

direction of work

resulting effect

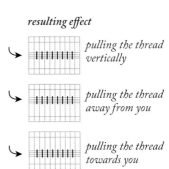

pulling the thread vertically

pulling the thread away from you

pulling the thread towards you

Pulled satin stitch fillings

- Simple parallel rows -

You can create a variety of fillings just by working rows of different heights, either directly adjacent to each other, or at varying distances apart, leaving 2 or 3 threads of the fabric between them, consistently or otherwise.

Always work from right to left and rotate the work 180° before you start on a new row.

You can obtain interesting effects by always pulling the thread flat along the fabric so that pairs of rows are pulled slightly towards each other (see sample 3).

worked using dentelle no. 80

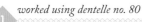

1

Here is our first set of rows of different heights. I have worked rows over 5, 4, 3 and 2 threads of the fabric: all combinations are allowed over a minimum of 2 threads.
This simple approach can be very useful for putting some final, interesting touches to a project.

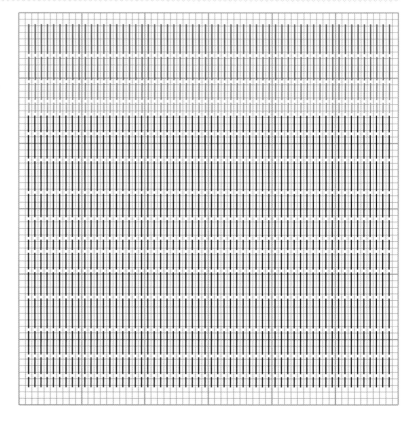

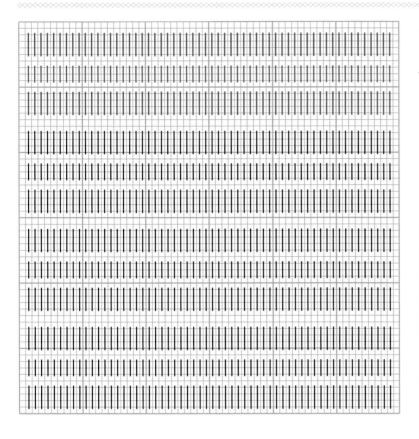

In this second set of rows, I have played around with how far apart the rows are set, leaving 1 or 2 threads of the fabric between them and making some rows over 3 threads and others over 4: use any combination you like when experimenting with these two aspects. This type of simple pattern is useful for making attractive borders.

worked using dentelle no. 80 3

The rows here are all of the same height, over 3 threads, and the stitches are pulled flat along the fabric, in opposite directions from one row to the next, creating larger gaps alternating with a pairs of rows that are closer together.

- Twice-stitched rows -

On a filling of parallel rows of the same height, the open areas can be re-embroidered, creating an infinite number of new patterns. Here are three examples, each worked with different threads.

4 *worked using cordonnet no. 100 on the top half and coton à broder no. 20 on the bottom half*

Work rows of pulled satin stitch over 4 threads with no gaps beween rows. Then work as shown in the diagrams below, working each horizontal stitch twice.

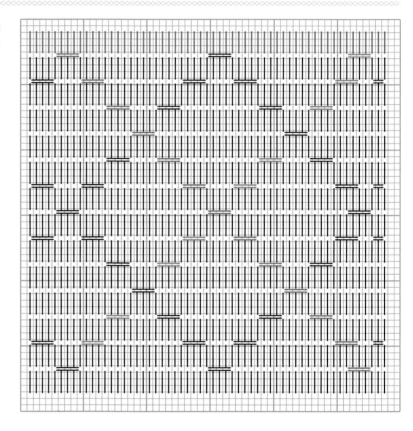

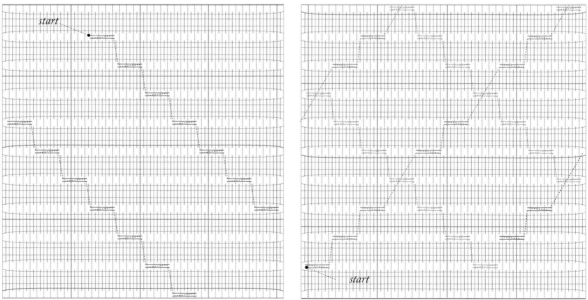

❶

❷

Rotate the work 180°

top half worked using cordonnet no. 100 and bottom half with coton à broder no. 30

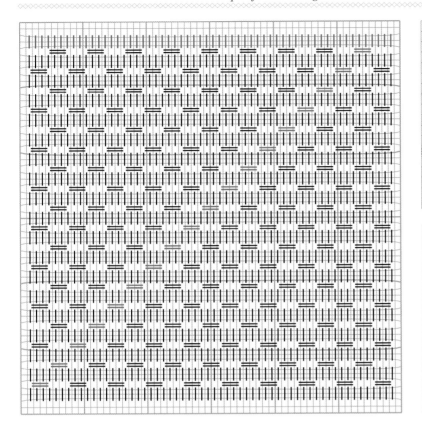

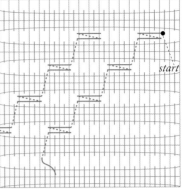

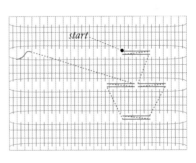

worked using dentelle no. 80

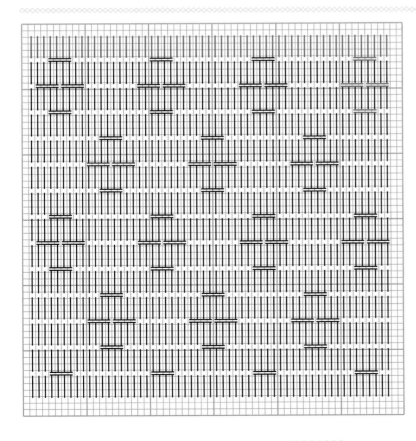

- Zigzags (step stitch) and chessboards -

These designs are created very simply in steps. The diagrams show how to work downwards. If working upwards, bring the thread out after the first block of stitches as shown in step 2.

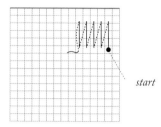

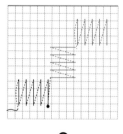

❶

Work an initial group of 5 pulled satin stitches over 4 threads of the fabric, bringing your needle out at the point shown.

❷

Rotate your work 90° clockwise and work a second group, bringing your needle out as shown. If you wish to work upwards, this will be how you finish your first block.

❸

Rotate your work 90° anticlockwise and work the third group like the first, continuing in the same way as you descend in steps.

 worked using dentelle no. 80

To create the chessboard effect, position the steps face to face. You can choose how dense you want to make the chessboard by varying the width of each block (by adding more stitches to each). You can also work the stitch over 3 or even 2 threads vertically.

This chessboard effect can be used on its own or as the basis for composite fillings.

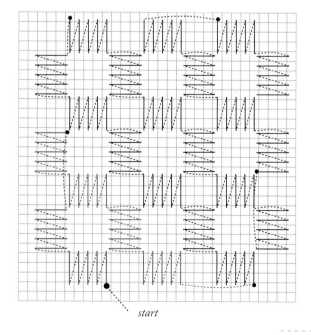

start

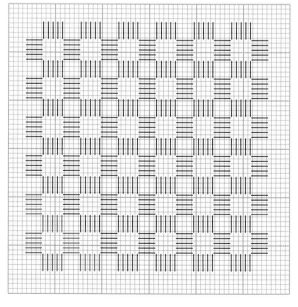

22

These designs are easy: just make sure no threads show through from the wrong side of the fabric by wrapping them tightly around the threads of the fabric when passing from one row to the next, and always work as shown.

worked using dentelle no. 80

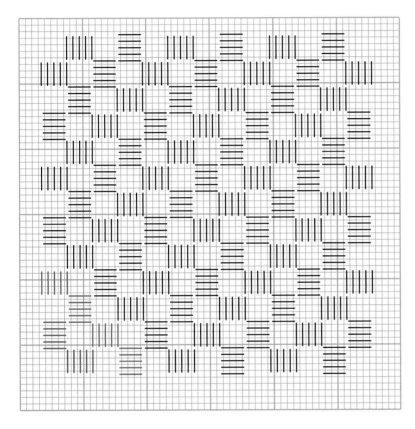

In this design, you can vary the width of each block (by adding more stitches to each). You can also work the stitch over 3 or even 2 threads. Another alternative is to leave 1 or 2 threads of the fabric between each row, which forms a different pattern, or alternate rows over 2 and 4 threads. Don't be afraid to experiment!

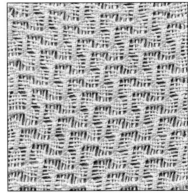

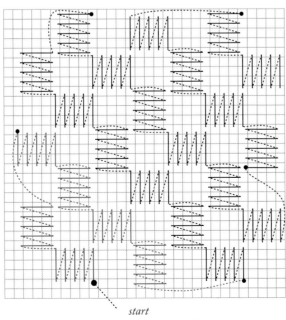

start

The two previous patterns combine well, especially if you play around with the height of the stitches: in this example some rows are worked over 2 threads and others over 4. Feel free to experiment with other patterns and threads.

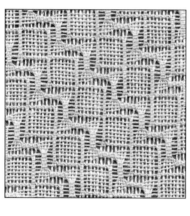

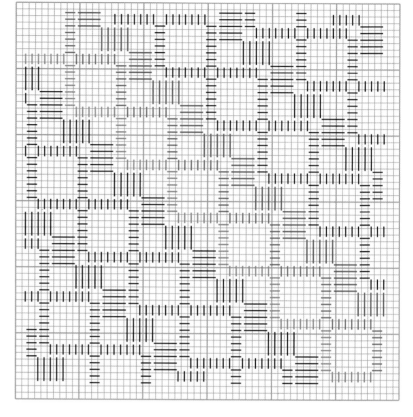

- Basket fillings -

These are classics of pulled thread embroidery. The basket fillings shown here are the ones used most frequently, with a few variations. You can seek inspiration in woven patterns or those of actual basketwork – they are often quite similar.

Three-strand basket fillings

Here are three examples of three-strand basket fillings, which will give you an idea of possible combinations. By varying the spacing between the blocks and the height of the stitches, you can achieve some very interesting results.

This is one of the best-known basket fillings: it is constructed using blocks of three parallel rows of pulled satin stitch as shown in the chart. You can also use small units of four, three-row blocks. It needs to be worked over a relatively large area for the pattern to come into its own.

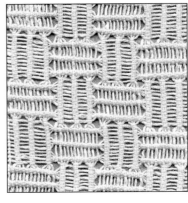

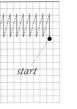 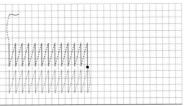 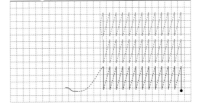

❶

Work an initial row of 13 pulled satin stitches over 4 threads of the fabric, bringing your needle out at the point shown.

❷

Rotate your work 180° and work the second row.

❸

Rotate your work 180° again to work the third row.

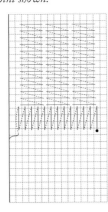 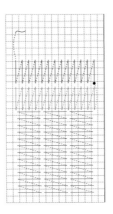

❹

Now rotate your work 90° anticlockwise and start the second block.

TIP:

Make sure you wrap the thread tightly round the threads of the fabric when you are passing from one row to the next, so they do not show through from the wrong side through the openwork you have created.

You can vary the number of threads you leave between the blocks of three rows, making them wider than they are tall; in this example there are 14 stitches, each over 3 threads.

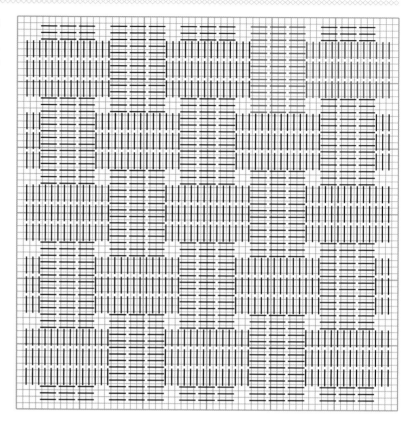

 worked using dentelle no. 80

You can also make bars of different heights within the same block; in this example there is one row of stitches over 6 threads between two rows of stitches over 3 threads.

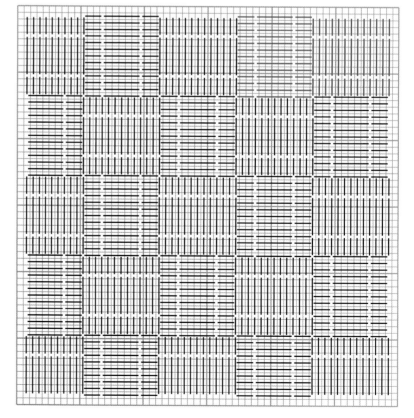

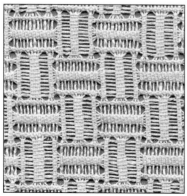

Two-strand basket fillings

As with the three-strand patterns, this can be worked with a variety of spacing. I have given two examples: one similar to the previous patterns, but leaving slightly larger areas unpulled, the other giving a more complex-looking weave without being overly difficult to work.

worked using dentelle no. 80

13

This pattern is embroidered over 4 threads, and the rows are 17 stitches wide.

❶

start

Work an initial row of 17 pulled satin stitches over 4 threads of the fabric, bringing your needle out at the point shown.

❷

Rotate your work 180° and work the second row.

❸

Now rotate your work 90° anticlockwise to work the next row.

❹

Rotate your work 180° again to work the second row of this block and bring your needle out at the point shown.

❺

Now rotate your work 90° clockwise and repeat from 1.

27

This version comprises blocks of two rows of 13 stitches worked over 3 threads. It creates a lovely twill-like pattern.

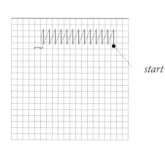

start

❶

Work an initial row of pulled satin stitches over 3 threads, bringing your needle out at the point shown.

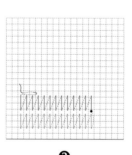

❷

Rotate your work 180° and work the second row.

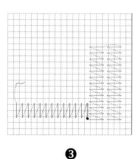

❸

Now rotate your work 90° anticlockwise to work the next row.

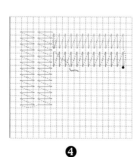

❹

Rotate your work 180° again to work the second row of this block and bring your needle out at the point shown.

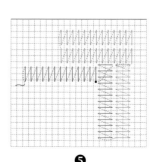

❺

Now rotate your work 90° clockwise and repeat from 1.

Single-strand basket stitches

Here are two classic fillings, both made from short, simply woven bars, followed by two less common designs that nonetheless create an interesting effect.

worked using dentelle no. 80

This design comprises simple, intersecting squares of 5 stitches worked over 4 threads: this design can also be used in stepped, diagonal formation or in small blocks of four bars.

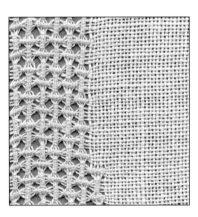

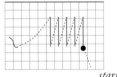

start

❶
Work an initial group of 5 pulled satin stitches over 4 threads, bringing your needle out at the point shown.

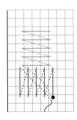

❷
Rotate your work 90° anticlockwise and work the second group.

❸
Now rotate your work 90° clockwise and repeat from 1. The bars on the second row will go in opposing directions to those on the first.

29

This is very similar to filling 15, but leaving one thread between each bar. Notice what a huge difference this small adjustment makes to the final result.

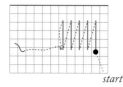

start

❶

Work a first group of 5 pulled satin stitches over 4 threads, bringing your needle out at the point shown.

❷

Rotate your work 90° anticlockwise and work the second group.

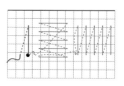

❸

Now rotate your work 90° clockwise and repeat from 1. The bars on the second row will go in opposing directions to those on the first.

Making the bars longer will give a less dense weave which can create an interesting effect, particularly with a slightly heavier thread. This is another chessboard design (similar to no. 7) that can also be used as part of a composite filling.
First work the horizontal rows, leaving 3 threads between them and staggering the bars; then rotate your work 90° and work the vertical rows in the same way.

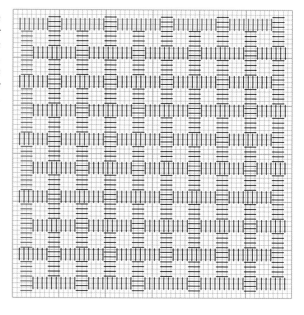

18

Here the bars are woven immediately adjacent to each other but staggered in both directions, forming a denser filling that, like other two- or three-strand basket fillings, works best when it covers a larger area.

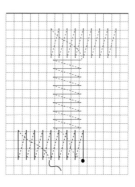

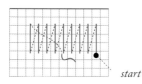

start

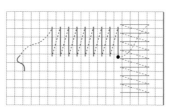

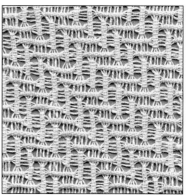

❶

Work a first group of 9 pulled satin stitches over 4 threads, bringing your needle out at the point shown.

❷

Rotate your work 90° clockwise and work the second group.

❸

Now rotate your work 90° anticlockwise and repeat from 1, and so on. The second row will intersect with the first, as shown on the chart.

Pulled satin stitch corners

- Embroidering corners -

When you change direction, you can embroider the corners fully or partially. If you want to fully embroider the corner (one stitch between each thread), you must use a fine thread so the stitches do not overlap and to ensure the corner is neat. Make sure you do not pull the stitches too tight at the corner: the threads of the fabric must be pulled taut, without puckering the fabric.

A different method is used depending on the direction in which you are working the corner, and both methods can be used when you are working in zigzag lines.

Turning downwards:

resulting effect

direction of work

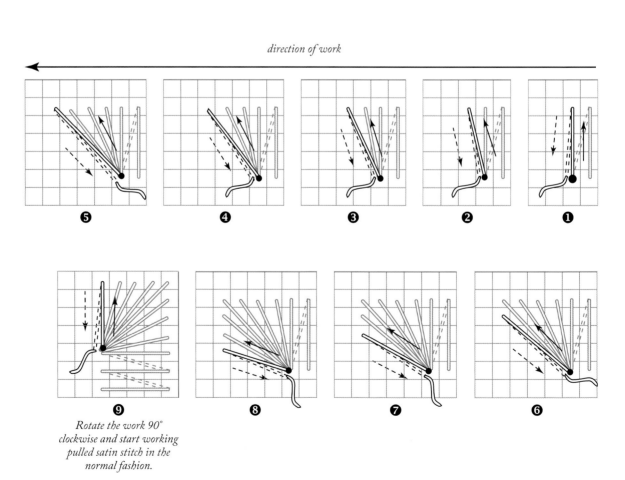

Rotate the work 90° clockwise and start working pulled satin stitch in the normal fashion.

Turning upwards:

resulting effect

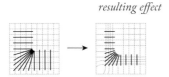

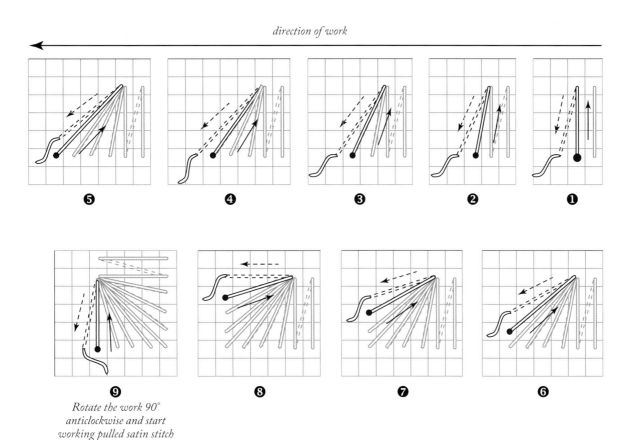

direction of work

❺ ❹ ❸ ❷ ❶

❾ ❽ ❼ ❻

*Rotate the work 90°
anticlockwise and start
working pulled satin stitch
in the normal fashion.*

When you are embroidering corners fully, you can use pulled satin stitch as a border and trim the fabric off to the row of stitches after ironing on the wrong side. For smaller works you will only need one row, or you can work several rows of the same or different widths, immediately adjacent to each other or with one or more threads in between, on their own or combined with other stitches. Note, however, this method of finishing will not work well on all fabrics: to check if you can use it on yours, embroider a few centimetres of pulled satin stitch on an off-cut or corner of fabric, then try to push the embroidered row along the fabric: if it holds well you can use this type of finish as a border, but if it slides along the threads, you will be better off with a hem (see page 12).

Once you can embroider lines and corners in pulled satin stitch, you can work all sorts of designs:
- patterns of squares, rectangles or spirals that can be used in single blocks or to create fillings, using pulled satin stitch on its own, or combined with other stitches.
- linear designs such as zigzags, crenellated or Greek patterns, rope and plait effects, and so on.

The previous technique creates dense stitching at the corner. For a lighter effect, you can just work a single diagonal stitch into the corner as follows:

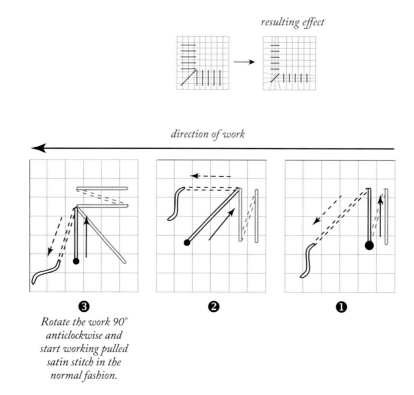

resulting effect

direction of work

❸

Rotate the work 90° anticlockwise and start working pulled satin stitch in the normal fashion.

❷

❶

Obviously this would not be sufficiently robust for the corner of a border. However, for fillings, the pattern formed is very different and gives an open, lacy effect.

- Linear patterns -

Opposite are two versions of the same pattern. The first is worked over 3 threads (corners made with a single diagonal stitch as above) and the second over 4 threads (corners fully embroidered, as explained on pages 32–33). The zigzag rows are immediately adjacent in the middle and spaced further apart on each side. All combinations are possible, as with simple pulled satin stitch, and you can create variations of the fillings shown here by varying the number of stitches used to work all or some of the corners.

worked using dentelle no. 80 (top right) and coton à broder no. 25 (bottom left)

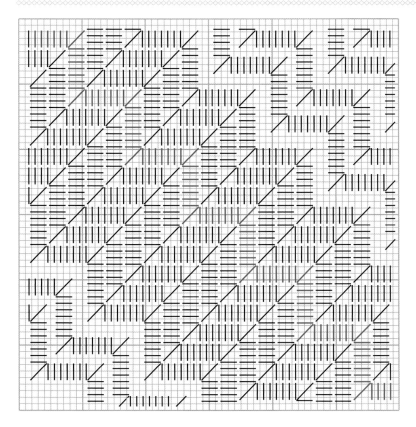

worked using dentelle no. 80

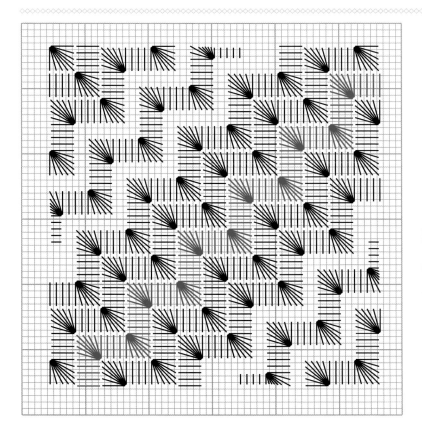

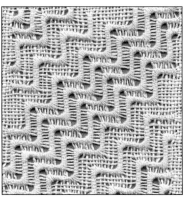

PULLED SATIN STITCH VARIATIONS

As stated previously, pulled satin stitch can be used in many ways. In particular, you can:

> leave spaces in the row of stitches
> vary the height of the stitches across the row
> stagger the blocks of stitches, keeping them the same height
> play with the spacing between the rows.

All these variations can be used as line stitches or fillings.

Spaced pulled satin stitch

An interesting effect can be achieved by leaving spaces in the rows of stitches at regular or irregular intervals: the non-embroidered parts form attractive undulating lines of open areas. This option is very good for fillings: by working adjacent rows you can form patterns, stripes or zigzags that stand out against the non-embroidered parts if you have spaced them at regular intervals. You can also leave non-embroidered parts at random intervals, for a different, more freeform effect.

- **Method** -

For this exmaple, work 7 pulled satin stitches over 4 threads, skip 6 threads then repeat. At the end of the row, bring your needle out at the point where you need to make the first stitch of the next row.

This stitch has many options, and you can play around with the number and size of the stitches as well as the spacing between the blocks of stitches (see samples 21–26). However, the non-embroidered areas should not be too large or too small to ensure that the background threads form a nice curve between the two blocks of stitches.

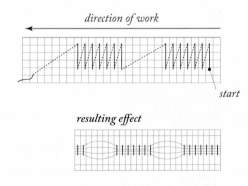

direction of work

start

resulting effect

worked using cordonnet no. 100

In this filling, the rows of 5 stitches over 4 threads are in a simple brick pattern.

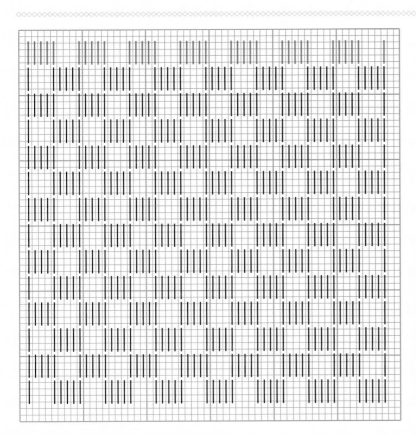

worked using dentelle no. 80

For this filling, the blocks of 6 stitches over 4 threads are staggered by a few stitches from one row to the next to obtain the effect of diagonal lines.

Staggering the pattern in one direction for a few rows, then in the other, forms a chevron design.

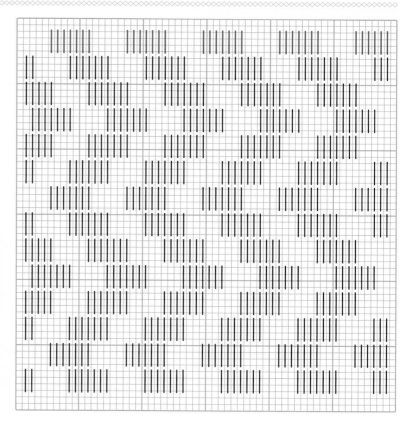

This pattern can be further enhanced as with the previous one by varying the size of the spaces in the basic line. Variations can also be made to the height of the blocks of stitches.

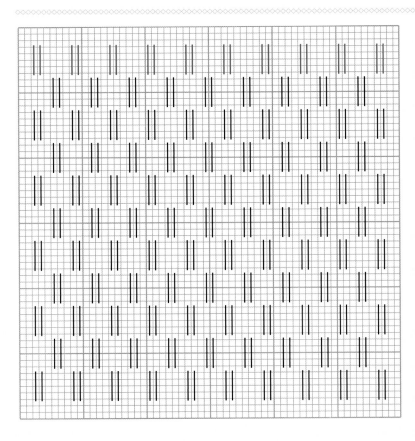

A completely different effect is achieved by working the stitches in groups of just two. Here, the groups of 2 stitches are separated by 5 threads, with no spaces between the rows, which are in a brick pattern.

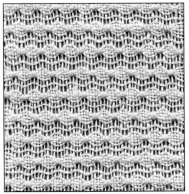

This filling is worked in the same way as the previous one, but leaving 1 thread between each row.

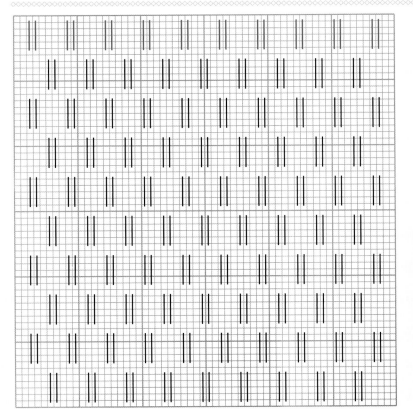

Varying the stitch height

- - - - - - - - - -

Lovely scalloped and arching patterns can be achieved by varying the height of the stitches along the row, resulting in different tensions being placed on the fabric threads. This technique can be used to make wavy lines, decorative bands or attractive fillings.

Here are a few examples:

- Satin stitch wavelet effect -

Work 6 pulled satin stitches over 4 threads, then 6 stitches over 2 threads, then another 6 stitches over 4 threads and so on, following the diagram.

You can make these 'wavelets' different sizes, but there must not be too many or too few of the shorter stitches, as this could prevent the threads of the fabric forming a nice curve above them.

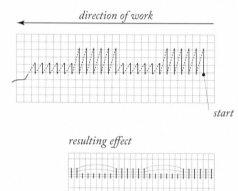

direction of work

start

resulting effect

27

This attractive filling is worked in staggered rows, so the stitches over 2 threads are worked under the stitches over 4 threads of the previous row.

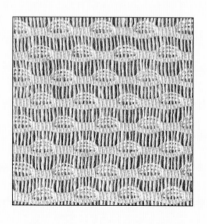

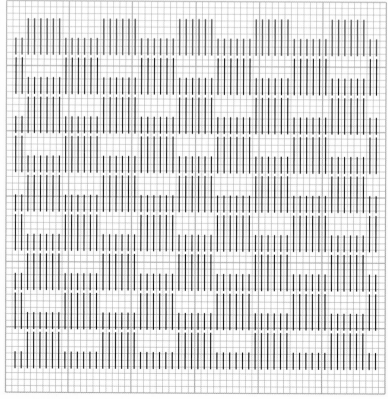

- Diamonds and other shapes in satin stitch -

Work the diamonds in pulled satin stitch as shown in the diagram, right, pulling tightly enough to bring the threads of the fabric closer together, without crushing the shape of the pattern. You need to adjust the tension on the thread depending on the stitch length, with the stitches becoming slacker the longer they get.

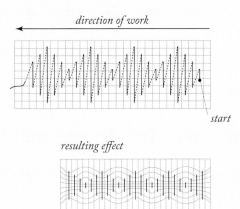

direction of work

start

resulting effect

worked using dentelle no. 80

Finer or heavier thread will also work. *This filling alternates rows of simple pulled satin stitch and rows of pulled satin stitch diamonds. As you can see in the chart, you can also create some attractive bands.*

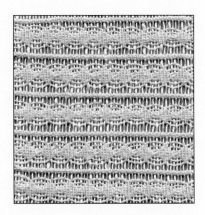

worked using coton à broder no. 30

You can use the technique described on page 41 to make other shapes such as these triangles, worked here in identical rows, all pointing in the same direction. From here, you can experiment with adjusting the stitch length and the layout of the rows.

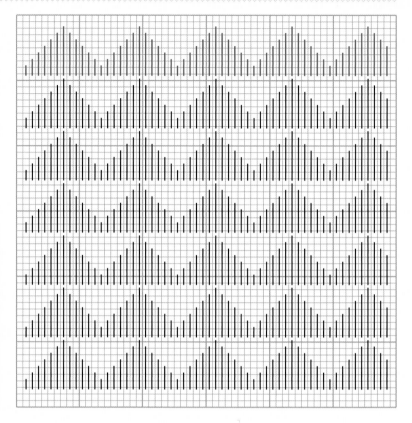

the triangles are worked in cordonnet no. 50 and the other rows in dentelle no. 80

Here is another lovely design, comprising triangles, wavelets and simple rows of pulled satin stitch.

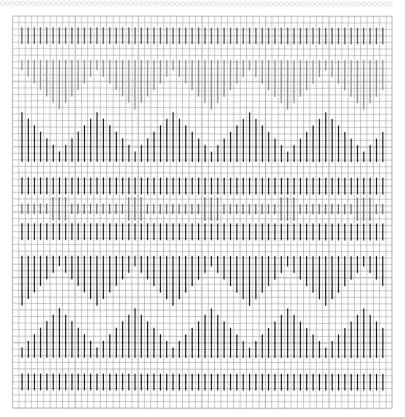

- Wave effect between rows -

A more elaborate technique can be used to create smooth curves formed by either the embroidered rows or the threads left unpulled.

worked using cordonnet no. 100

In this first filling, 2 threads have been left between the rows, and these threads form attractive waves moving smoothly from one row to the next.

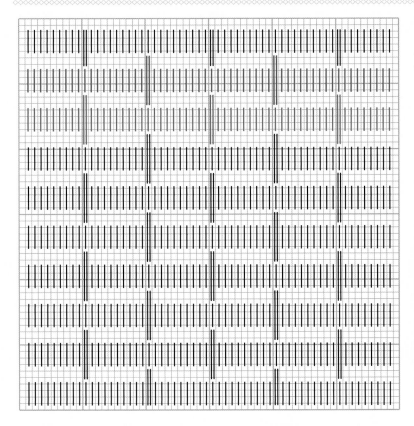

❶

First work 9 satin stitches over 4 threads, then bring your needle out an extra 2 threads lower down to make 2 stitches over 8 threads in the same place; then continue as shown on the diagram, working 19 small stitches, followed by 2 large ones, to the end of the row.

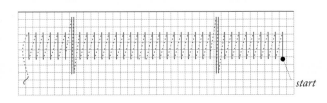

start

❷

Rotate the work 180° and repeat the first row in an identical fashion, but staggering the large stitches. Make sure that at the end of each row you bring your needle out in the right place to start the next row.

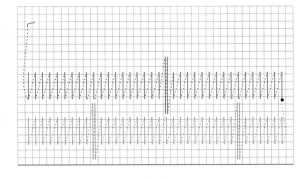

❸

Continue in the same way until you reach the end of the pattern; then work the last row as shown in the chart above to ensure a neat finish.

Here the whole area is embroidered, alternating one row over 4 and 8 threads with one row over 2 and 8 threads. Note that in the first and last rows the longer stitches are over 6 threads. The waves formed are a little more rigid as they are held tight in the stitches.

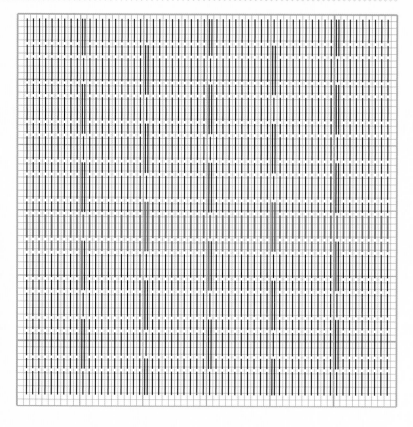

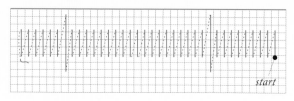

❶ *First work 9 satin stitches over 4 threads, then bring your needle out an extra 2 threads further down and make 1 stitch over 8 threads; then continue as shown in the chart, working 19 small stitches, followed by 1 large one, and so on.*

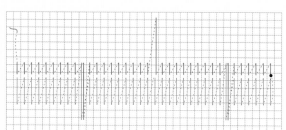

❷ *Rotate the work 180° and work the second row with the small stitches over 2 threads and the large ones over 8; the large stitch will be worked over the long stitch of the previous row every other time.*

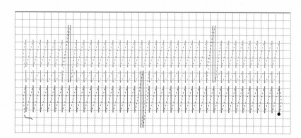

❸ *Rotate the work 180°. Return to working over 4 and then 8 threads, but this time start with 19 small stitches. Work row 2 again and then return to row 1 to begin the pattern again. Work the first and last rows as shown in the chart for a neat finish.*

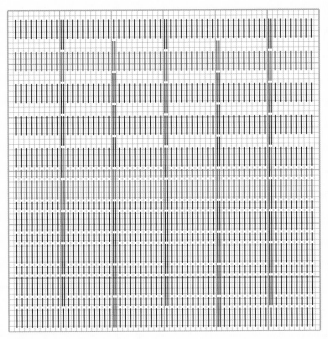

Here is a second version of the same stitch combination. Why not combine the different options in one filling?

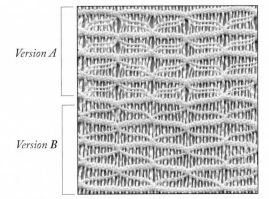

Version A

Version B

Method – version A:

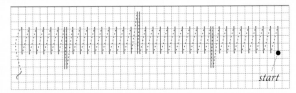

start

❶ First work 9 satin stitches over 4 threads, then bring your needle out an extra 2 threads further down to work 2 stitches over 6 threads in the same place; then continue as shown, working 9 small stitches, followed by 2 large ones, which will alternate upwards and downwards.

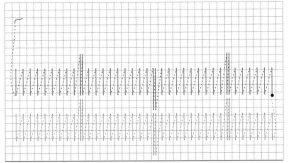

❷ Rotate the work 180° and repeat the next row in the same way. Make sure that at the end of each row you bring your needle out in the right place to start the next row.

❸ Continue in the same way until you reach the end of the area you want to fill, then work the last row as shown on the diagram to ensure a neat finish.

Method – version B:

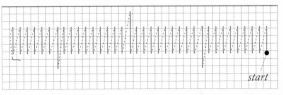

start

❶ First work 9 satin stitches over 4 threads, then bring your needle out an extra 2 threads further down to make 1 stitch over 6 threads; then continue as shown on the diagram, working 9 small stitches and 1 large one, which will alternate upwards and downwards.

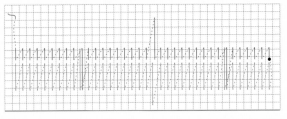

❷ Rotate the work 180° and work the second row with the small stitches over 2 threads and the large ones over 6: the large stitch will be worked over the equivalent stitch in the previous row every other time.

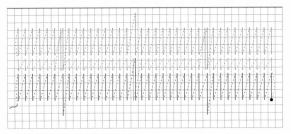

❸ Continue to the end of the pattern, alternating these two rows; then work the last row as shown on the diagram to ensure a neat finish.

Staggering stitches of the same height

You can create attractive waves by using stitches of the same height but staggering the blocks by one or more threads upwards or downwards. Work as previously in horizontal lines, which can be used as bands or fillings.

Work 6 pulled satin stitches over 4 threads, then bring out your needle an extra 2 threads further down and work another 6 stitches over 4 threads; work the next block 2 threads higher up, repeating this pattern until the end of the row.

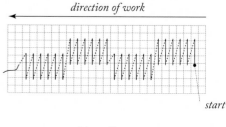

direction of work

start

resulting effect

worked using cordonnet no. 100

34

In this filling, the basic row is formed of blocks of 6 stitches over 4 threads, worked as shown above. All the rows are the same and are worked in an identical fashion.

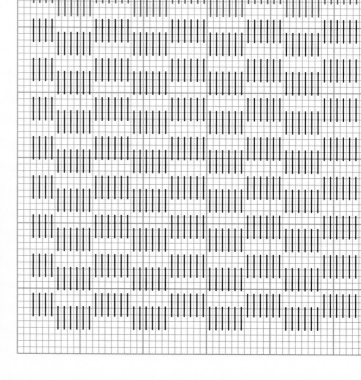

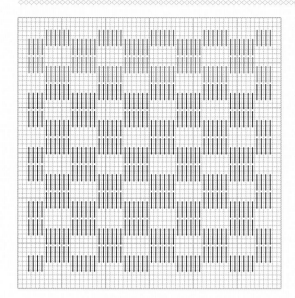

Here the basic rows are the same as in the previous example, but are spaced symmetrically so there are two groups of stitches immediately adjacent to each other.

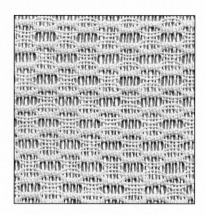

You can also stagger the blocks of stitches by one or more threads upwards or downwards, but always in the same direction; you will then work in diagonal rows. If you are using this method, leave 2 threads between each row, to form a filling of delicate wavelets.

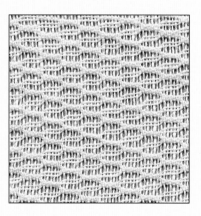

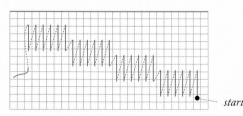

start

❶ *Work 6 pulled satin stitches over 4 threads, then start the next block 2 threads higher up, and work another 6 stitches over 4 threads; repeat until the end of the row. At the end of the row, bring out your needle at the point where you need to make the first stitch of the next row, leaving 2 threads between the rows.*

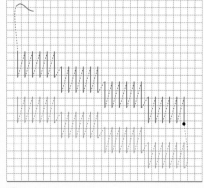

❷ *Rotate the work 180° and work the second row in the same way, following the chart.*

With some patterns, it doesn't matter whether you work horizontally or diagonally.

37 *worked using cordonnet no. 100*

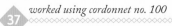

In this example, the rows interlock and the pattern made by the fabric threads in the previous patterns disappears, replaced by an elongated honeycomb design.

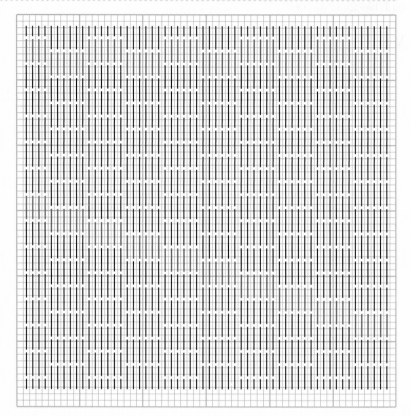

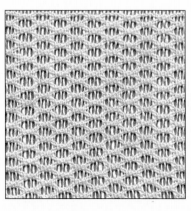

38 *worked using cordonnet no. 100*

This pattern is very similar to the previous one, and the way it is worked is the same; there are just fewer stitches in each block (4 instead of 6), leaving 2 threads between each group. The honeycomb effect is slightly altered: rounder and more open.

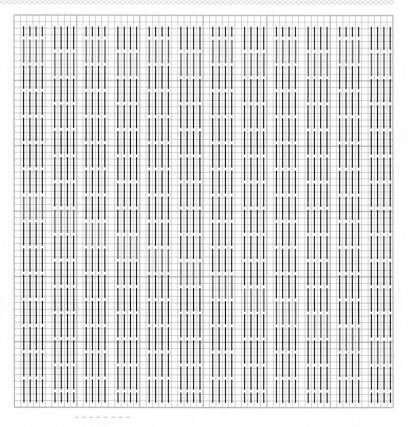

- Subdividing the blocks -

A line of relatively tall stitches over 6 threads can be separated into two or three narrower lines, which then revert to the initial height, then separate again, and so on. The subdivision can occur at regular or random intervals and both blocks of stitches can vary in length.

Method – subdividing into three:

 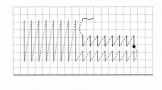

start

❶

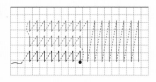

❷

❸

For example, work 8 pulled satin stitches over 6 threads, then 8 stitches over 2 threads, pulling tightly, and bringing your needle out as shown on the diagram. Of course you can work with a different number of stitches.

Rotate the work 180° and work 8 stitches over the 2 threads in the middle, making sure that you continue to pull tightly.

Rotate the work 180° again (you are back at your starting point) and work 8 stitches over the remaining 2 threads, continuing to pull tightly. Repeat from 1, and continue in the same way, following the diagram.

You can obtain a whole range of fillings using this basic combination but altering the ratio of the blocks and using a brick pattern, staggering the rows or arranging them randomly. Here are a few examples; if you experiment you will find many others. You can also leave 1 or 2 threads between the rows, and so on.

worked using cordonnet no. 100

39

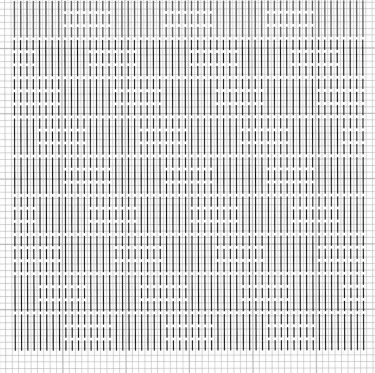

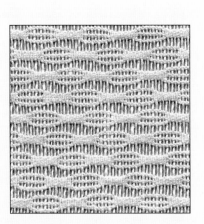

Staggering the rows by just a few stitches will produce a striped effect. For a chevron effect, you need to stagger a few rows in one direction, then a few rows in the other and so on (see pattern 23 on page 38).

Method – subdividing into two:

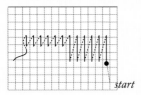

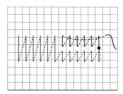

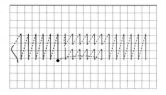

❶

Work 6 pulled satin stitches over 4 threads, bring out your needle 2 threads down (instead of 4), and work 6 stitches over 2 threads; bringing your needle out at the base of your last stitch.

❷

Rotate the work 180° and work another 6 stitches over 2 threads; bring your needle out at the point shown on the diagram, weaving your thread through the stitches that you have just worked.

❸

Rotate the work 180° again and repeat from 1.

◆ **40** *worked using coton à broder no. 20*
~~~~~~

By dividing the line into just two, and stitching with a rounder, heavier thread, the outcome is different once again. There are many options for using these new patterns.

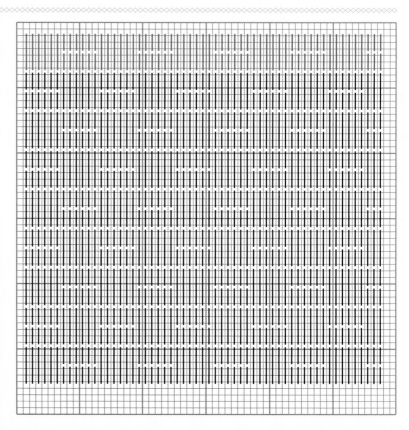

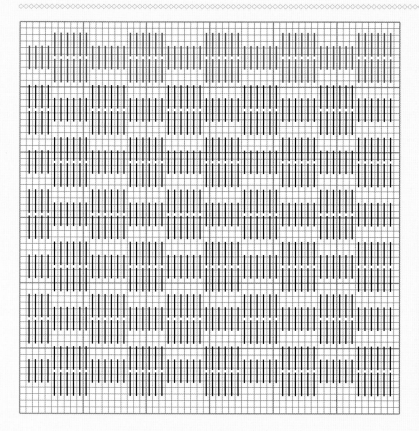

If you keep the same stitch height throughout but still alternate between one and two rows, it is then the line itself that changes in height, forming a totally different pattern where, once again, a wavelike pattern is formed.

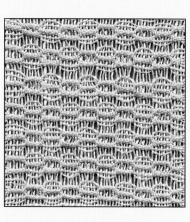

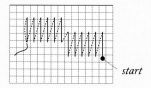

→ *start*

❶

Work 6 pulled satin stitches over 4 threads, bring out your needle 2 threads down (instead of 4), and work another 6 stitches over 4 threads, bringing your needle out at the base of your last stitch.

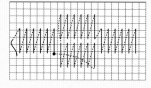

❷

Rotate the work 180° and work another 6 stitches over 4 threads; bringing your needle out at the point shown on the diagram.

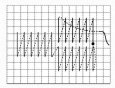

❸

Rotate the work 180° again and repeat from 1.

Your pattern can now become more
complex: the line can branch off several
times as it gets larger, then return to its
initial size.

Traditionally, these patterns are used for
fillings. A fine thread is generally used, and
the stitches pulled tightly; alternatively
they can be embroidered using satin stitch
in a heavier thread, without pulling.

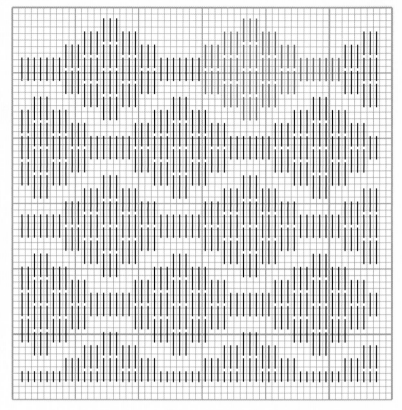

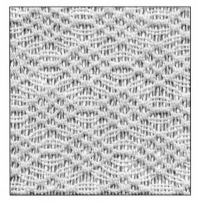

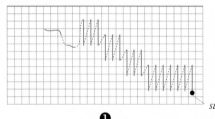

❶

start

Work 7 pulled satin stitches over 4 threads, bring out your needle
2 threads down (instead of 4) and work 3 stitches over 4 threads,
then repeat to work two more staggered blocks of 3 stitches. Come
out finally as shown, weaving your thread through the threads of
the fabric.

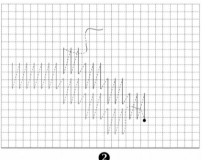

❷

Rotate the work 180° and this time work four groups of
3 stitches as shown. Bring your needle out as shown, weaving
your thread under the stitches that you have just worked.

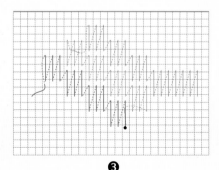

❸

Rotate the work 180° again and work another four groups of 3
stitches in the same way, bringing your needle back out at the base
of your last stitch.

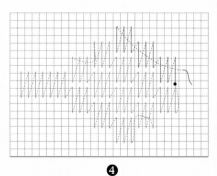

❹

Rotate the work 180° once more and this time work three
groups of 3 stitches in the same way; bring your needle out as
shown, weaving your thread under the stitches that you have
already worked. Rotate the work 180° again and repeat from 1.

Satin stitch version worked using coton à broder no. 20

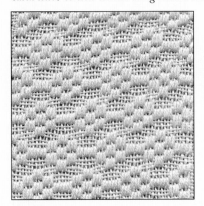 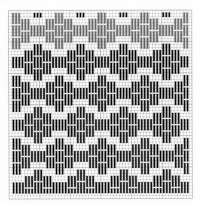

Numerous pulled satin stitch designs can be combined with traditional satin stitch for attractive fillings: lozenges, triangles and basketwork-effect, for example. It is well worth experimenting with composite fillings using these two techniques. Here are some examples of suitable satin stitch patterns taken from 18th century embroidered lace.

Satin stitch worked with three strands of stranded cotton

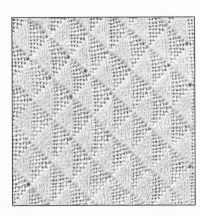 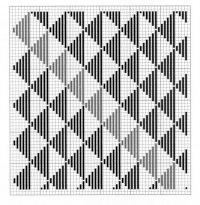

Satin stitch worked with three strands of stranded cotton

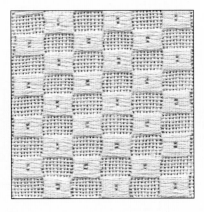 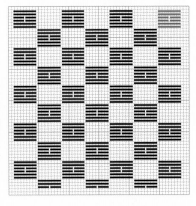

DIAGONAL PULLED SATIN STITCH

Method

Diagonal pulled satin stitch is easier than it looks. When used to create a band, it is mostly combined with straight pulled satin stitch or eyelets to create small composite blocks. When used for a filling, it is rarely used alone, but it is sometimes combined with other pulled thread stitches to make diagonal patterns (version 1, in particular); it results in very attractive, uniform fillings when combined with eyelets (version 2, generally). It is worked upwards from right to left, using an average weight of thread, pulling hard to create the 'holes' in the fabric.

VERSION 1:
Can also be worked over 2 threads

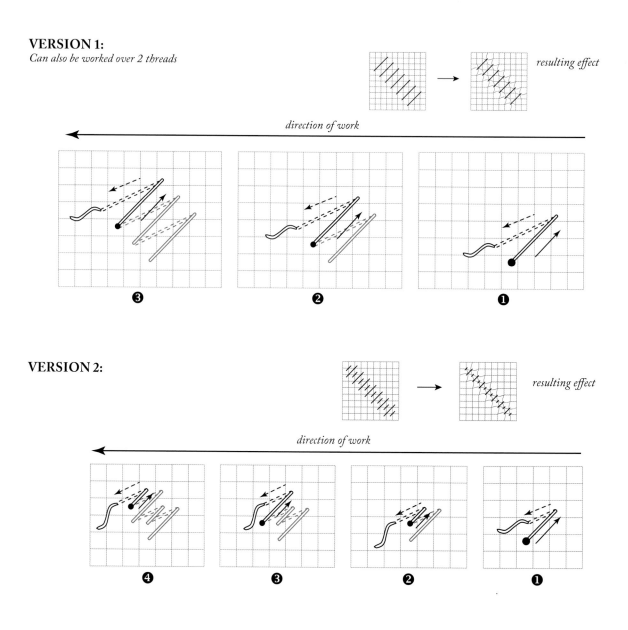

resulting effect

direction of work

❸   ❷   ❶

VERSION 2:

resulting effect

direction of work

❹   ❸   ❷   ❶

- Corners -

When you want to change direction, to create a diamond or a zigzag with a worked corner, for example, you should proceed as follows:

VERSION 1:

Can also be worked over 2 threads

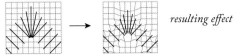

resulting effect

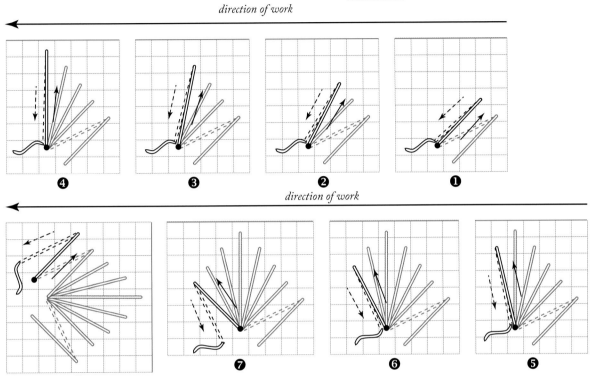

Rotate the work and start working pulled satin stitch again in the normal fashion.

VERSION 2:

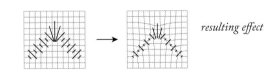

resulting effect

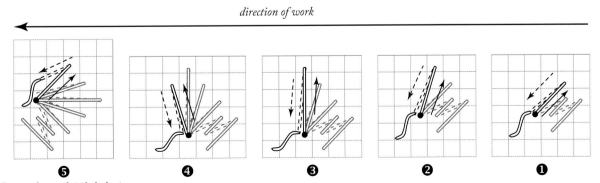

Rotate the work 90° clockwise and start working pulled satin stitch again in the normal fashion.

Diagonal pulled satin stitch fillings

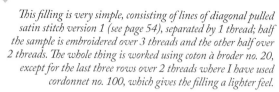

43 *worked using coton à broder no. 20*

This filling is very simple, consisting of lines of diagonal pulled satin stitch version 1 (see page 54), separated by 1 thread; half the sample is embroidered over 3 threads and the other half over 2 threads. The whole thing is worked using coton à broder no. 20, except for the last three rows over 2 threads where I have used cordonnet no. 100, which gives the filling a lighter feel.

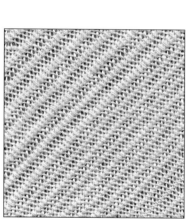

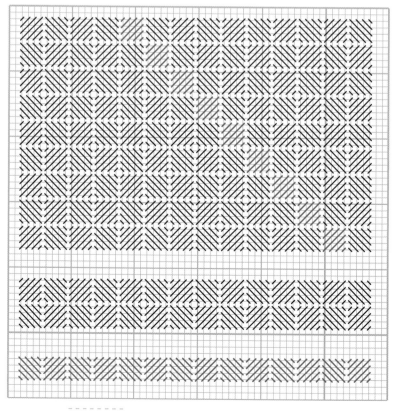

44 *worked in coton à broder no. 20 on the left-hand side, with cordonnet no. 50 top right and no. 30 at the bottom*

Here is a very elegant filling; it is a satin stitch pattern worked diagonally, but with a pulled stitch wrapping the threads tightly at the point. It can be used to form single or double lines. It is most impressive when worked with a round, fairly heavy thread: coton à broder no. 20 or 25 for example, or cordonnet no. 50. See the instructions opposite.

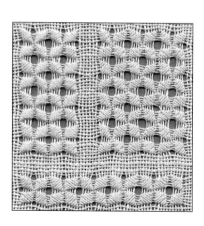

There are two different ways of approaching design 44, depending on whether you are creating a simple line or filling an area. For a simple line, proceed as follows:

direction of work

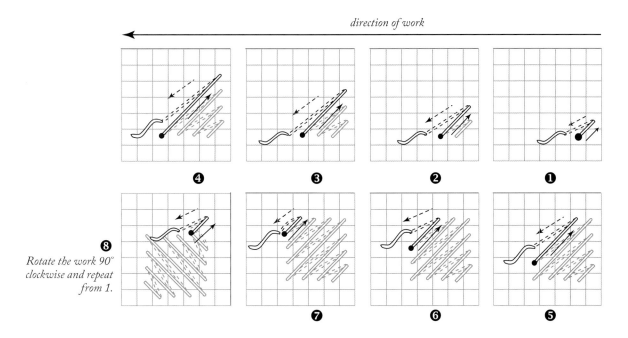

❹ ❸ ❷ ❶

❽
Rotate the work 90° clockwise and repeat from 1.

❼ ❻ ❺

For a double line or larger filling, it is much quicker and simpler to work the rows diagonally and bring the needle out again as shown in 7:

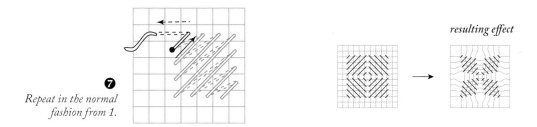

❼
Repeat in the normal fashion from 1.

resulting effect

worked with coton à broder no. 25

 45

Here is a magnificent version of this filling, obtained by leaving one thread between each block of stitches. Follow the instructions above, working diagonally, but at 7 bring your needle out as shown:

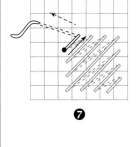

❼

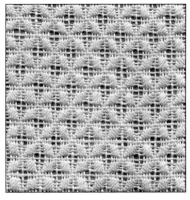

FOUR-SIDED STITCH

Four-sided stitch is widely used and easy to work. The lines are lighter and less pronounced than when you use pulled satin stitch. It is useful for forming different fillings on its own or in combination with other stitches. It can also be used to make attractive picot edgings.

FOUR-SIDED STITCH

Method

- Working horizontally -

Choose the weight of your thread based on the effect you want to achieve: the finer the thread, the lighter and more lace-like the look of the embroidery. It is worked from right to left over 2, 3 or 4 threads, pulling hard on the thread.

Four-sided stitch can be used on its own as line stitch or in larger linear patterns, on its own or with pulled satin stitch for a border, for example; it can even be used with pulled satin stitch on the same line, at varying intervals. It also creates an easy filling, on its own or combined with other stitches. **Note:** although this is called four-sided stitch, you only work three sides of each square as the first side of the next square completes the previous square.

- Corners -

When you use four-sided stitch as a line stitch, and need to change direction, you should pay particular attention to how you work the corners; you need to embroider the two outside stitches of the corner before rotating your work and setting off again as normal.

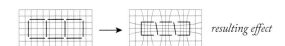

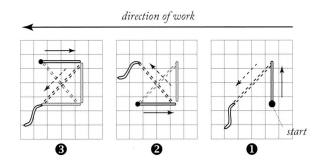

resulting effect

direction of work

❸   **❷**   **❶**   *start*

Turning downwards:

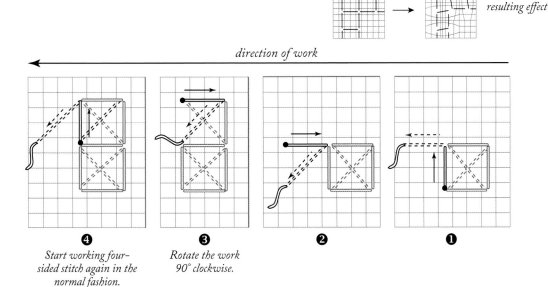

resulting effect

direction of work

❹
Start working four-sided stitch again in the normal fashion.

❸
Rotate the work 90° clockwise.

❷   **❶**

Turning upwards:

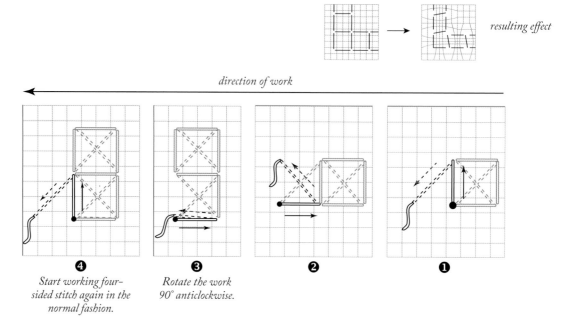

direction of work

❹

Start working four-sided stitch again in the normal fashion.

❸

Rotate the work 90° anticlockwise.

❷

❶

resulting effect

- Working vertically -

Four-sided stitch can also be worked vertically, as follows. This forms two adjacent horizontal stitches which can be very useful in certain patterns.

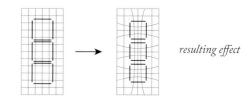

resulting effect

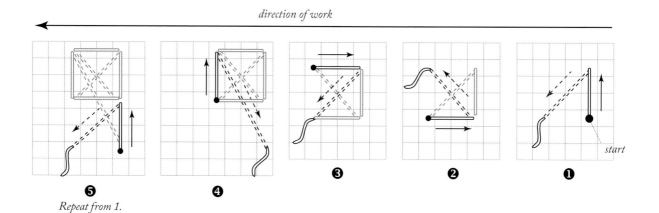

direction of work

❺

Repeat from 1.

❹

❸

❷

❶

start

60

- Working diagonally -

The instructions below explain how to work four-sided stitch on the diagonal:

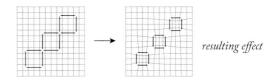

resulting effect

direction of work

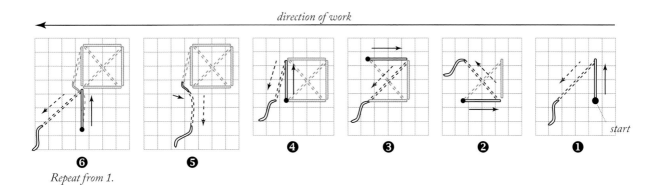

❻

❺

❹

❸

❷

❶

start

Repeat from 1.

Four-sided stitch can be worked in a single diagonal row, in bands or changing directions.

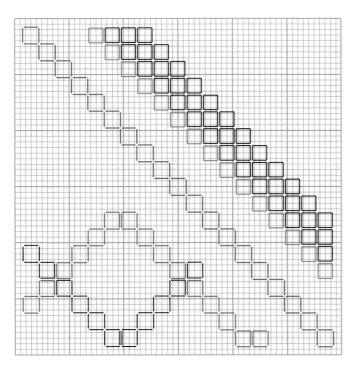

worked in coton à broder no. 30

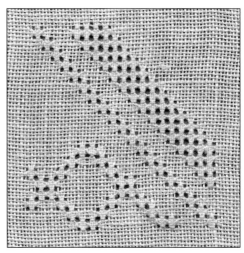

Fillings using horizontal four-sided stitch

Four-sided stitch on its own can be used to form several fillings, depending on how successive rows are spaced in relation to each other.

worked using dentelle no. 80

46

Successive rows worked immediately adjacent to each other form a regular, rather plain, mesh-like grid, which can complement more elaborate work.

This filling is quite easy to work: at the end of each row, rotate the work 180° to start the next row immediately adjacent to the first.

It can be worked over 2, 3 or 4 threads.

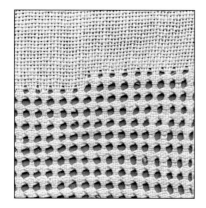

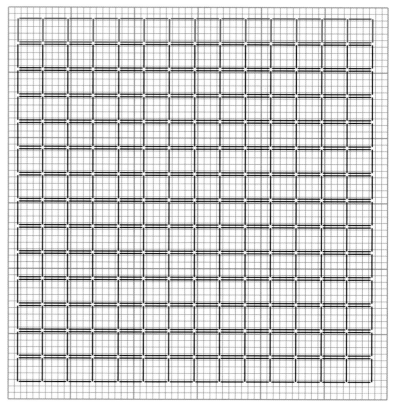

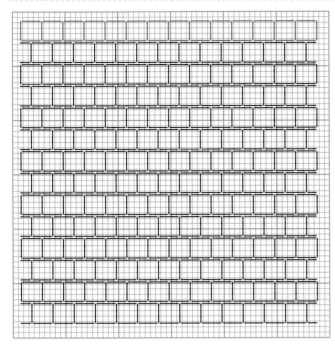

If you work over an even number of threads (generally 4), preferably using a fine thread, you can embroider successive rows in a brick pattern. This results in a narrow row of attractive openwork with alternating diagonal threads behind.

As stitches are staggered between rows, you need to start the second row with an incomplete stitch, as shown on the diagram.

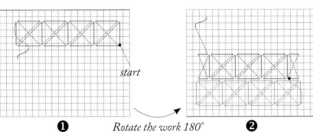

start

❶   *Rotate the work 180°*   **❷**

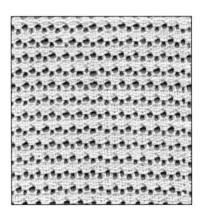

As long as you work over an even number of threads, you can combine side-by-side rows and rows in a brick pattern to achieve a more varied filling.

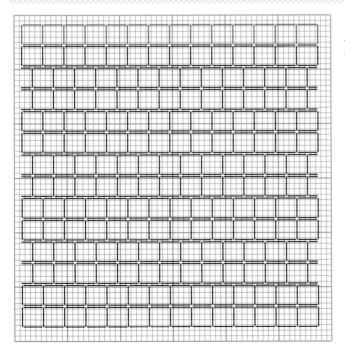

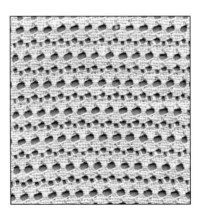

When you are staggering the rows, you can also leave 1 (A) or 2 (B) threads between the rows, to create yet another pattern.

A.

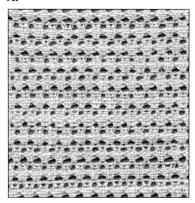

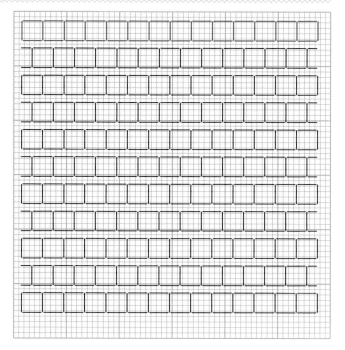

B.

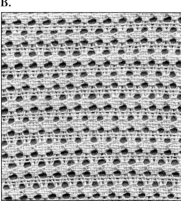

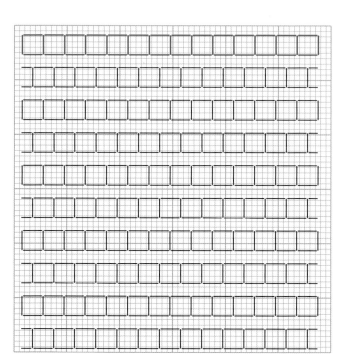

It is interesting to combine the different possibilities, alternating rows in different forms – side-by-side and a brick pattern, leaving 1 or 2 threads in between, and so on.

Composite fillings can look great when they combine rows of different stitch sizes; this can normally only be done by stitching over even numbers of threads: one row of stitches over 4 threads and one or two rows over 2 threads for example.

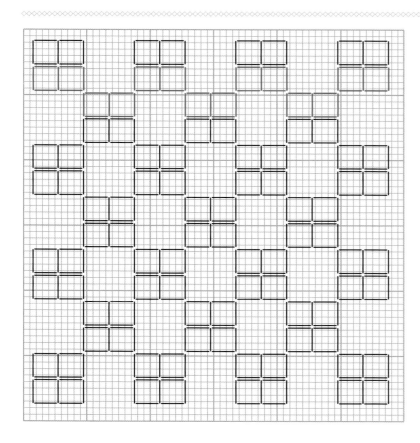

For this filling, the four-sided stitches are in blocks of four. It is worked by alternating between two levels and positioning the rows symmetrically and immediately adjacent to each other.

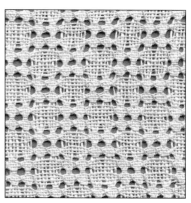

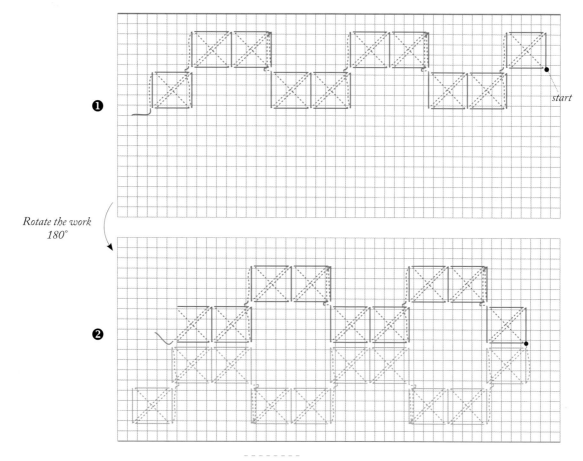

❶

start

Rotate the work 180°

❷

SPACED FOUR-SIDED STITCH

Method

Four-sided stitch can be worked in single squares that are spaced apart from each other, as follows:

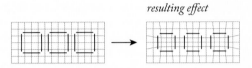

resulting effect

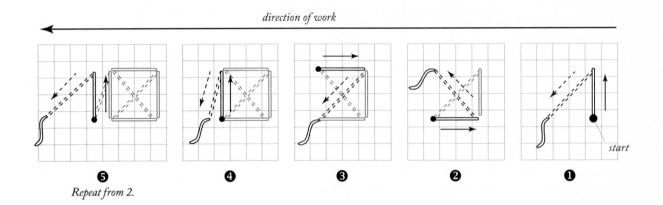

direction of work

❺

Repeat from 2.

❹

❸

❷

❶

start

These single squares can be worked in single rows or as fillings. They are mainly used to form 'window' fillings like the ones shown opposite, either with a single cross, as in sample 51, or a double cross, as in sample 52.

Fillings using spaced four-sided stitch

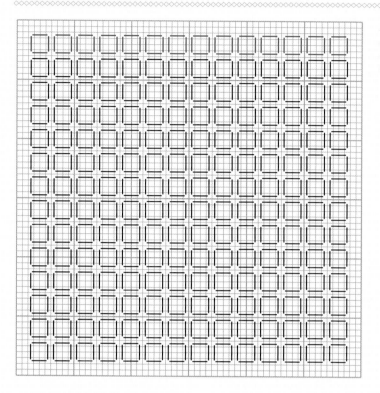

Here is an attractive, yet easy filling that creates the effect of single-cross windows. At the end of each row, rotate your work 180° to start the next row, leaving one thread between each row.

For a filling of double-cross windows, leave 2 threads between each square and 2 threads between each row.

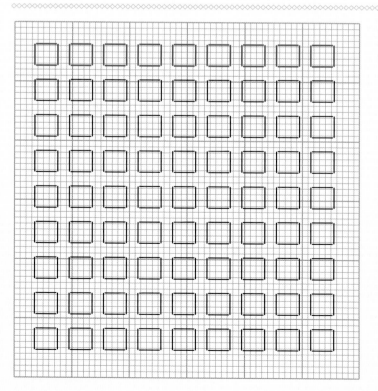

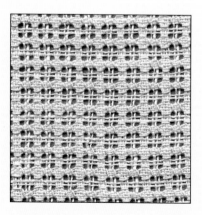

DIAGONAL FOUR-SIDED STITCH

Method

- The basic stitch -

The diagonal four-sided stitch forms a line that is well structured but does not created a particularly open effect. It can be used on its own as a line stitch, but is better worked as a filling, on its own or in combination with other stitches.

A thread of average weight will give the most attractive result.

It is worked over 2 or 3 threads, **from left to right,** moving upwards, pulling hard on the thread to open out the 'holes' in the fabric.

resulting effect

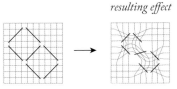

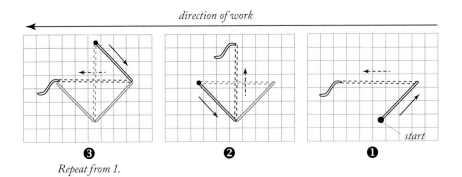

direction of work

❸   **❷**   **❶** *start*

Repeat from 1.

- Corners -

When using diagonal four-sided stitch as a line stitch, if you need to change direction, you must pay particular attention to the corners: as with straight four-sided stitch, you need to embroider the two outside stitches of the corner before rotating your work and setting off again as normal.

resulting effect

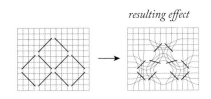

direction of work

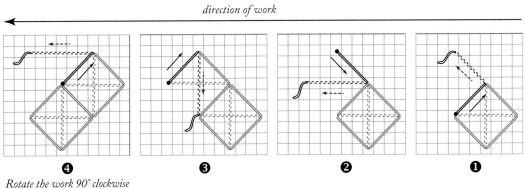

❹   **❸**   **❷**   **❶**

Rotate the work 90° clockwise and start working again in the normal fashion.

Fillings using diagonal four-sided stitch

Diagonal four-sided stitch is very versatile for fillings:
- successive rows with no threads in between form a regular grid, which is slightly different from the one made using straight four-sided stitch;
- if you leave one or more threads between the rows, you get a strongly diagonal filling;
- you can also combine single and double rows, for example, to achieve a more varied finish;
- you can work rows that cross each other, forming a grid pattern of small or large holes.

Start with the central row and work to one side first, and then the other.

worked using dentelle no. 80 53

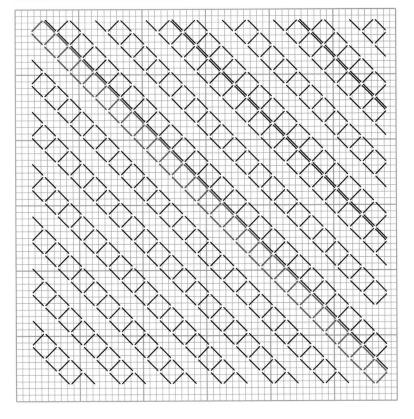

In this sample, the rows of stitches over 2 threads are spaced as shown; single rows are used at bottom left and alternating single and double rows at top right.

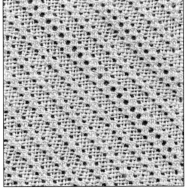

Work all the diagonal rows in one direction and then those at right angles. This example is quite dense, but you can make it looser by spacing the rows further apart, still in multiples of two if you are working your stitches over 2 threads as here, or in multiples of three for stitches over 3 threads.

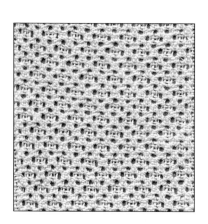

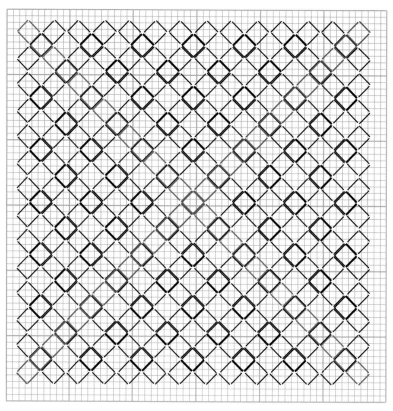

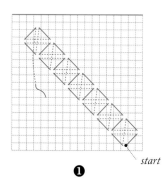

❶

Work an initial row of diagonal four-sided stitch, bringing your needle out as shown to work the second row 4 threads from the first.

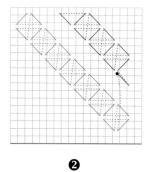

❷

Rotate your work 180° and work the next row in parallel in the same way, 4 threads from the first; continue in the same way until you have covered the required area.

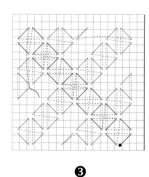

❸

Rotate your work 90° anticlockwise and start again in the opposite direction, using the same technique.

REVERSE WAVE STITCH

Reverse wave stitch is widely used and very easy. It creates light, airy bands, meshes and window fillings. Like four-sided stitch, it can be worked in different directions and it combines well with other stitches.

REVERSE WAVE STITCH

Method

- The basic stitch -

Reverse wave stitch is worked over 2, 3 or 4 threads horizontally and over an even number of threads vertically, generally two or four. Choose the weight of your thread based on the effect you want to achieve: the finer the thread, the lighter and more lace-like the result. This stitch is worked from left to right, pulling hard on the thread.

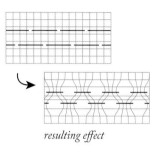

resulting effect

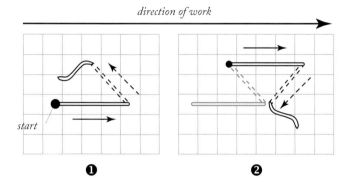

direction of work

start

❶   ❷

To work two immediately adjacent rows, proceed as follows:

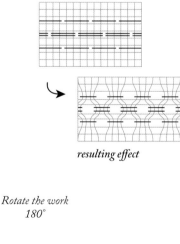

resulting effect

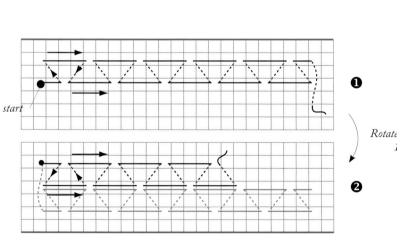

start

❶

Rotate the work 180°

❷

73

- Corners -

When you use reverse wave stitch as a line stitch, and you need to change direction, you should pay particular attention to how you work the corners: you need to embroider the two outside stitches of the corner before rotating your work and setting off again as normal.

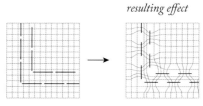

resulting effect

Turning upwards:

direction of work

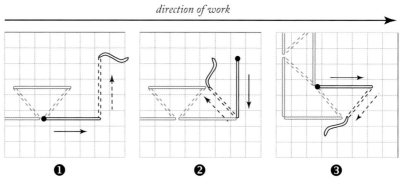

❶   ❷   ❸

Rotate the work 90° clockwise and start working again in the normal fashion.

Turning downwards:

direction of work

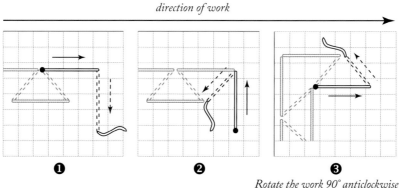

❶   ❷   ❸

Rotate the work 90° anticlockwise and start working again in the normal fashion.

Note: to make working corners easier, I would advise working over 2 threads vertically and forming the stitch over 4 threads, as shown on the diagram, or over 3 threads vertically for a stitch length of 6 threads. In all other cases, you will need to decrease the length of the inside or outside stitch in the corner so you still have the same stitch height after you have turned (see cable stitch, page 78).

Fillings using reverse wave stitch

Used on its own, reverse wave stitch creates simple, vertical/horizontal or slightly diagonal fillings, which can provide areas of simplicity within a design and highlight more elaborate areas of stitchwork. Once again, experimenting with stitch height will reap rewards.

worked using cordonnet no. 50 **55**

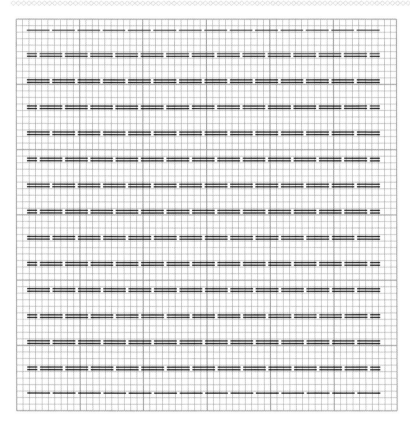

In this first filling, the stitches are worked over 4 threads, and the rows are immediately adjacent, as explained on page 73. This works best if the thread is not too fine.

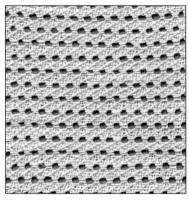

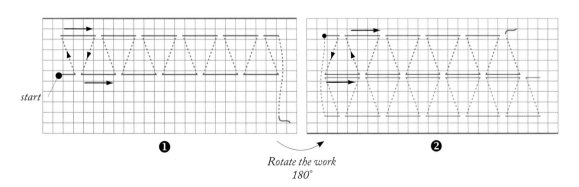

start

❶

Rotate the work 180°

❷

For this grid pattern, the stitches are worked as on page 73, but 4 threads are left in between each row. The work is done in two stages; all the horizontal rows first, then you rotate the work to start on the vertical rows and complete the grid. It works best with a round, fairly fine thread.

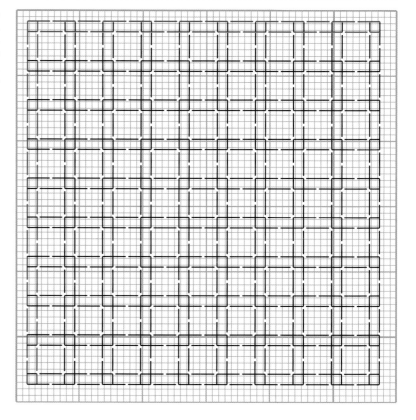

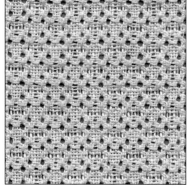

start

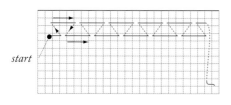

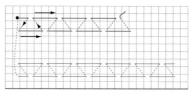

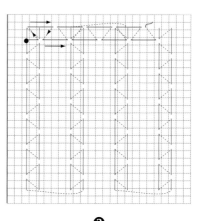

❶

Work the first row, then come out as shown on the diagram.

❷

Rotate your work 180° and work the second row, continuing in the same way until you have covered the required area.

❸

Now rotate your work 90° clockwise and continue in the same fashion to complete the grid.

worked using dentelle no. 80

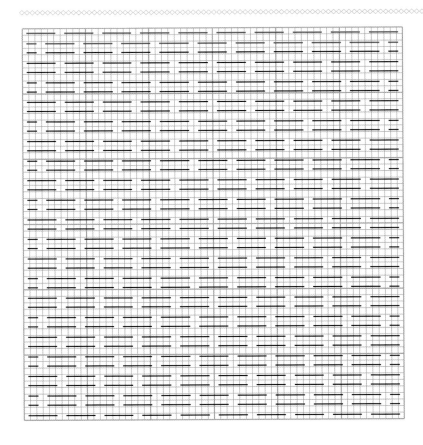

Reverse wave stitch makes an attractive
window filling if you work the stitch
over an odd number of threads (here 5
horizontally and 2 vertically) and leave
1 thread in between each row.

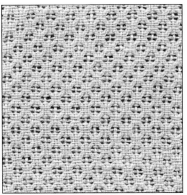

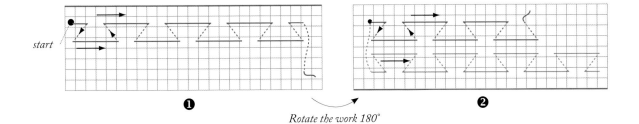

start

❶

Rotate the work 180°

❷

CABLE STITCH

Method

- The basic stitch -

This is a flattened version of reverse wave stitch that is only one thread high. Like reverse wave stitch, it can be worked in two or more immediately adjacent rows, or combined with other stitches. Opt for a thread of middling thickness to highlight the sturdy effect, while not detracting from the openwork appearance. Like reverse wave stitch, it is worked from left to right, pulling hard on the thread. (See the sample on page 80.)

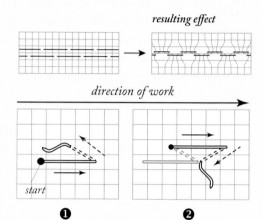

resulting effect

direction of work

❶   ❷

Cable stitch is always worked in double rows, to obtain the cable-like effect. The adjacent rows are worked in the same way as reverse wave stitch, with a stitch height of one thread:

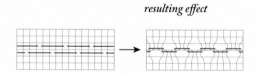

resulting effect

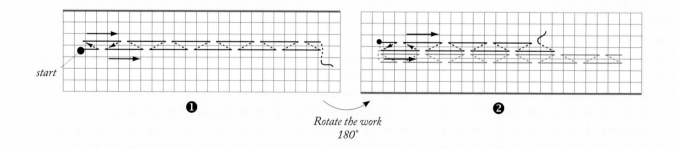

start

❶   ❷

*Rotate the work
180°*

- Corners -

As with reverse wave stitch, when you are using cable stitch as a line stitch and need to change direction, you must embroider the 2 outside stitches of the corner before rotating your work and setting off again as normal. However, as the stitch is only 1 thread high, you will have to work your last stitch, and the first stitch following it, over 3 threads instead of 4.

Turning upwards:

resulting effect

direction of work

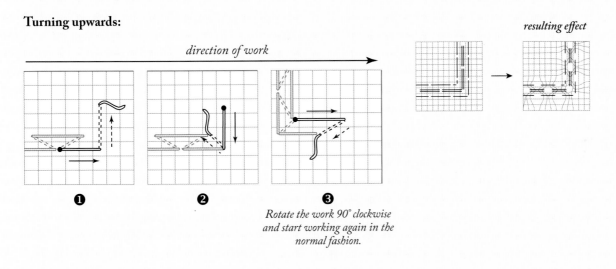

❶   ❷   ❸

Rotate the work 90° clockwise and start working again in the normal fashion.

Turning downwards:

resulting effect

direction of work

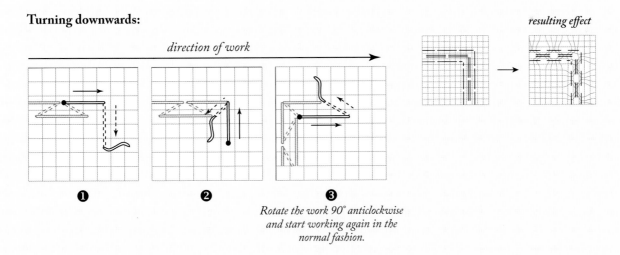

❶   ❷   ❸

Rotate the work 90° anticlockwise and start working again in the normal fashion.

Alternatively, instead of making the outside stitches longer at a corner, you could make the inside stitches shorter: it is up you to choose which suits your work better.

Cable stitch filling

worked with coton à broder no. 20

This is a simple filling, using a variety of spacings between the bands. It is worked here in bands of two and four rows.

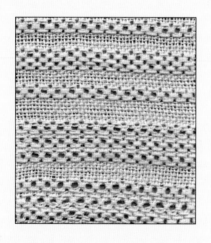

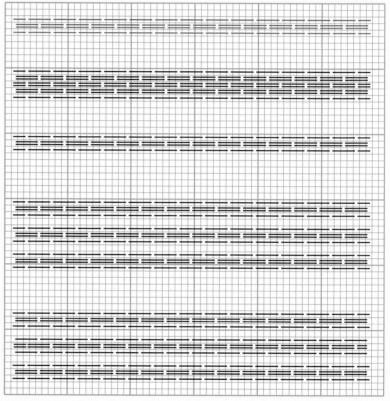

80

REVERSE FAGGOT STITCH

Method

- **The basic stitch** -

Just like reverse wave stitch, but worked on the diagonal, reverse faggot stitch is fairly easy to work. Whether you are using it in single or double lines, the effect is very attractive and can be used to create some elegant zigzag patterns. It is a great filling stitch, on its own or combined with numerous other stitches, and is worked over 2, 3 or 4 threads depending on the effect you want to achieve and how fine the fabric is.

Choose the weight of your thread based on the effect you want to achieve: the finer the thread, the lighter and more lace-like the work will look. It is stitched from left to right, upwards, pulling hard on the thread.

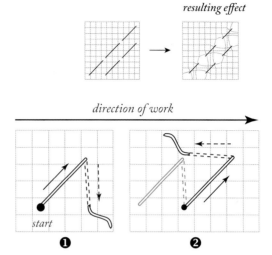

resulting effect

direction of work

❶   ❷

start

To work two adjacent rows, proceed as in the diagrams, right:

The chart below is for the sample beside it.

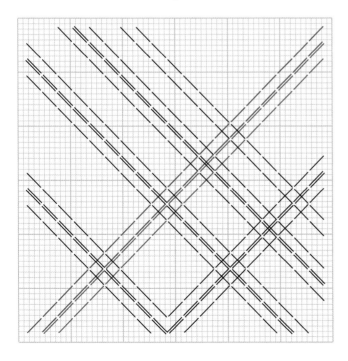

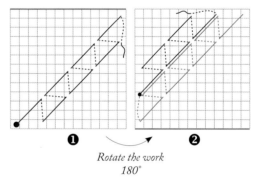

❶   ❷

*Rotate the work
180°*

worked using dentelle no. 80

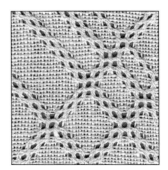

- Corners -

When you are using reverse faggot stitch as a line stitch, and need to change direction, you need to work the two outside stitches of the corner before rotating your work and setting off again as normal.

Turning upwards:

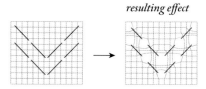

resulting effect

direction of work

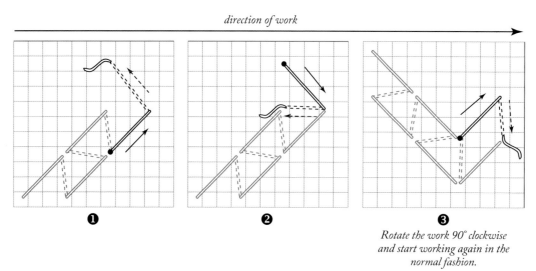

❶ ❷ ❸

Rotate the work 90° clockwise and start working again in the normal fashion.

Turning downwards:

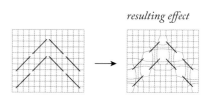

resulting effect

direction of work

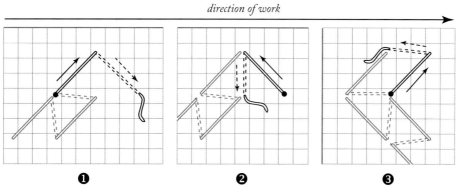

❶ ❷ ❸

Rotate the work 90° anticlockwise and start working again in the normal fashion.

Fillings using reverse faggot stitch

Even used on its own, reverse faggot stitch can create fillings that range from simple to elaborate. Rows can be worked in a single direction to form a horizontal/vertical grid filling if the rows are touching, or a strongly diagonal pattern if stitch characteristics are varied: lines of single or double stitches, different spacing between rows, and so on. It is also possible to embroider two crossing layers of stitches, forming more textured patterns of varying degrees of complexity.
Start with the central row and work to one side first, and then the other.

worked using dentelle no. 80

Here are two fillings in one: the top right corner is formed of rows that run immediately adjacent to each other in the same direction, while the bottom left corner is formed of two crossed layers of reverse faggot stitch in adjacent rows.

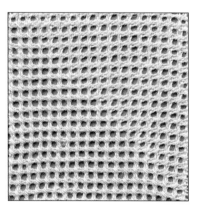

Top right corner:
Work the adjacent rows side-by-side, rotating your work 180° for each new row until you have filled the required area.

Bottom left corner:
Having worked stages 1 and 2, rotate your work 90° anticlockwise, and work at right angles to the previous rows in the same way.

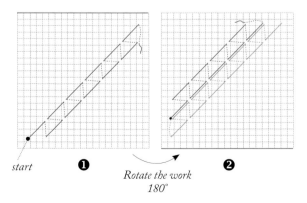

start ❶ *Rotate the work 180°* ❷

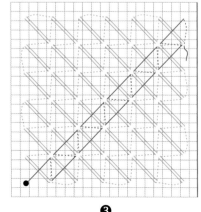

❸

By spacing the rows further away from each other and working two crossed layers again, you obtain a latticework design, which creates a very attractive grid filling. Here, I have embroidered single rows of stitches over 3 threads, 6 threads apart. With reverse faggot stitch over 2 threads, you only need to space the rows 4 threads apart to achieve the same pattern, or 6 or 8 threads apart for a more open latticework.

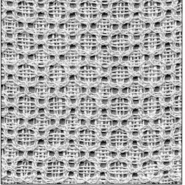

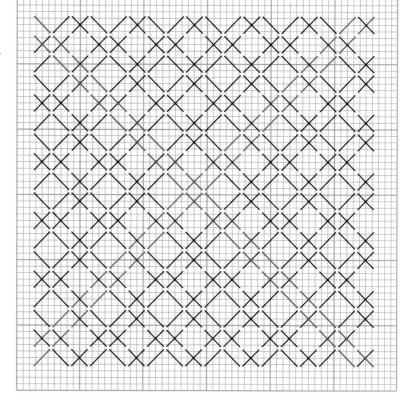

Start with the central row and work to one side first and then the other. You only begin the rows at right angles once you have worked all those in the first direction. Pay close attention to the spacing of the rows if you are not working to a set design – it is not always easy to tell where you have got to.

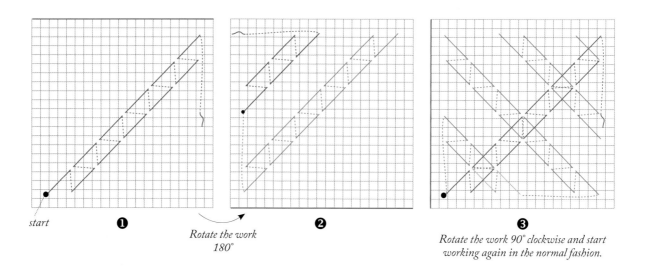

start ❶

Rotate the work 180°

❷

❸

Rotate the work 90° clockwise and start working again in the normal fashion.

worked using dentelle no. 80

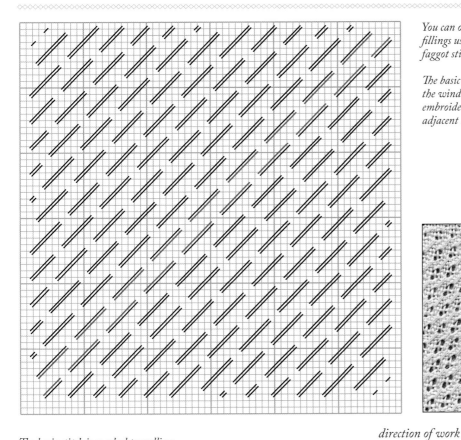

You can obtain some attractive window fillings using a variant of reverse faggot stitch.

The basic stitch is slightly different and the window effect appears when you embroider several rows immediately adjacent to each other.

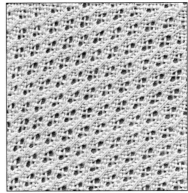

direction of work

The basic stitch is worked travelling upwards from left to right:

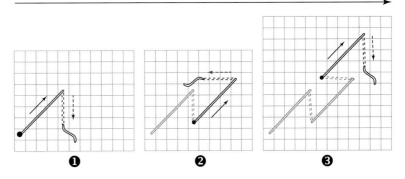

❶   ❷   ❸

As is the case with the majority of fillings, you need to rotate your work 180° at the end of each row to start on the next.

Start at the centre of your pattern and work adjacent rows on one side, as shown on the diagram. Then work the second half of the pattern in the same way.

Note: as you are working diagonally, you need to think carefully at the start of each new row how long the first stitch should be to maintain the pattern; you will often need to work ¼, ½ or ¾ stitches.

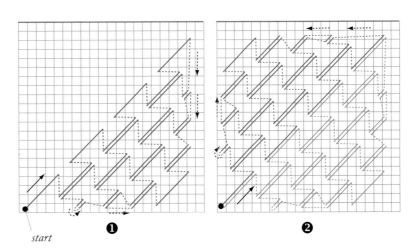

start

❶   ❷

85

WAVE STITCH

Wave stitch is exactly the same as reverse wave stitch (see previous chapter) but effectively the back of the fabric becomes the front. Although rarely used as a single line stitch, it is sometimes used as a double line for a very light, eyelet effect. It is a good stitch for creating horizontal/vertical or diagonal grid fillings, and the effect it produces varies hugely depending on the number of threads over which it is worked.

WAVE STITCH

Method

- The basic stitch -

Wave stitch is worked over 2, 3 or 4 threads vertically, and 2, 3 or 4 threads horizontally. Each stitch is worked diagonally but the row is worked horizontally across the fabric. A fine thread is preferable in this case as it will enhance the lightness of the stitch.

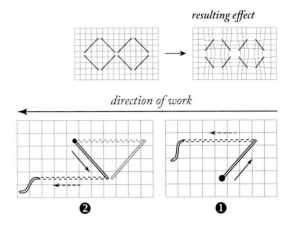

resulting effect

direction of work

Work from right to left, pulling hard on the thread:

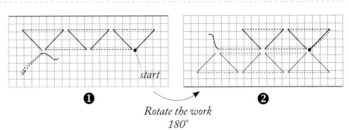

start

Rotate the work 180°

- Variation -

The spacing between stitches can produce the effect of small, single eyelets or single- or double-cross windows (see samples 64 and 65). For small, single 'eyelets', work as follows: the first two stitches as normal, then the next two spaced further away, depending on the density you wish to achieve. Then rotate the work 180° and work the second row in the same way, with the double stitches effectively mirroring those in the first row.

For single-cross windows, work in the same way, leaving one thread between the first two stitches and one thread between the two rows. For double-cross windows, leave 2 threads between the first 2 stitches and 2 threads between the two rows.

These options can create a fairly horizontal/vertical filling, or be used with other stitches for fillings with more of a diagonal movement.

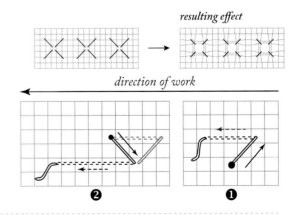

resulting effect

direction of work

To work two adjacent rows, follow the diagrams, right:

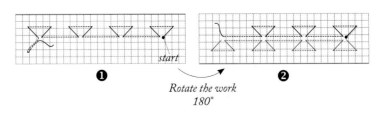

start

Rotate the work 180°

Fillings using wave stitch

When used on its own, wave stitch usually creates fillings of fairly horizontal/vertical grids, the appearance of which varies depending on the number of threads crossed horizontally and vertically. This is demonstrated in these next two fillings, which are worked in the same way, but over a different number of threads.

 worked using dentelle no. 80

In this pattern, each stitch is worked over 3 threads horizontally and vertically.

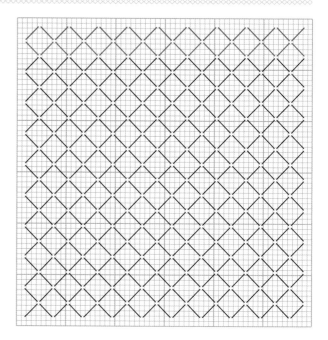

 worked using dentelle no. 80

In this second pattern, the stitches are worked over 2 threads horizontally and 4 vertically to create a more open mesh.

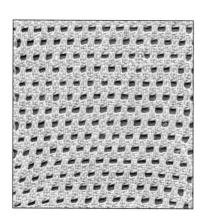

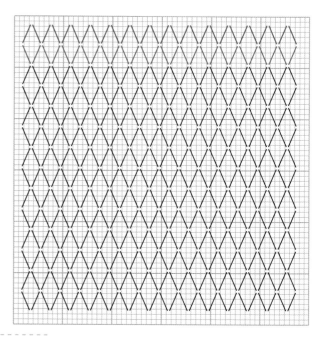

As with reverse wave stitch, you can use wave stitch to create attractive, very light window fillings by spacing the stitches and rows 1 or 2 threads apart.

worked using dentelle no. 80

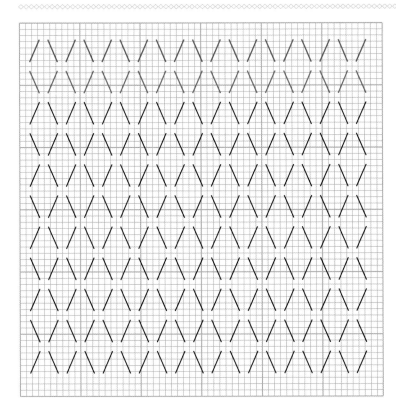

For this filling, each stitch is worked over 2 threads horizontally and 4 threads vertically, leaving 1 thread between each stitch and 1 thread between each row. This creates a single-cross window pattern.

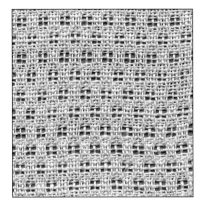

worked using dentelle no. 80

By leaving 2 threads between each stitch and 2 between each row, you create a double-cross window filling.

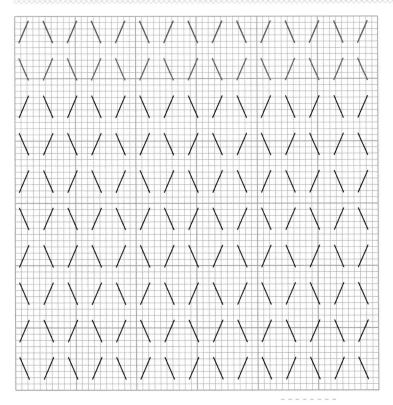

FAGGOT STITCH

Method

- The basic stitch -

Faggot stitch is like a diagonal form of wave stitch. It is as easy as wave stitch, and even more commonly used; it is generally worked in single or double lines, creating fillings on its own or in combination with other stitches to form a very light background. As with wave stitch, it forms a double line of well-defined 'holes'. It is worked over 2, 3 or 4 threads, preferably using a fine thread so the lightness of the stitch is emphasized.

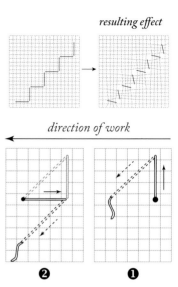

resulting effect

direction of work

❷   ❶

- Variations -

By increasing the spacing between stitches, you can produce a very light effect of windows or crossed windows. Lines of small windows, generally worked over 2 threads, can form very light fillings on their own, or be used in combination with other stitches for fillings with slightly more pronounced patterns. Crossed-window effects need to be worked over 3 or 4 threads to create proper interest; they also form very attractive fillings, which can be found on the traditional headdresses and clothing of several regions of France: it is well worth visiting even the smallest of regional museums to see if you can find any treasures!

For a mesh-like effect, work as shown below: the first two stitches normally, then the next two further on, depending on the density you wish to achieve. Rotate the work 180° and work the second row in the same way, with the double stitches effectively mirroring those in the first row.

For single-cross windows, you simply need to leave one thread in both directions between the two rows, which can be worked normally or by spacing the groups of two stitches apart from each other, as before.

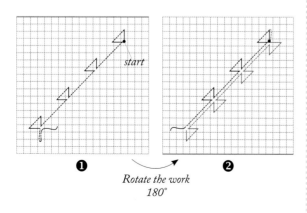

❶   ❷

Rotate the work 180°

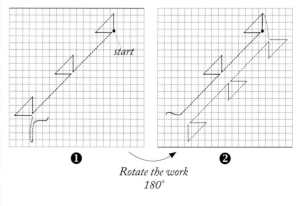

❶   ❷

Rotate the work 180°

Fillings using faggot stitch

Faggot stitch forms very light fillings on its own, in rows worked at varying distances apart, but can also be combined with other, more solid stitches, either to make a new pattern, or to provide the pattern with a simple background. Start with the central row and work to one side first and then the other.

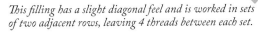

worked using dentelle no. 80 **66**

This filling is very light and comprises adjacent rows of faggot stitches worked over 4 threads.

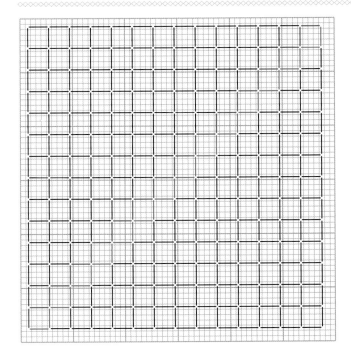

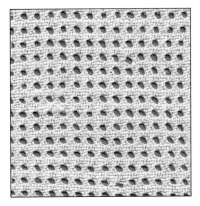

worked using dentelle no. 80 **67**

This filling has a slight diagonal feel and is worked in sets of two adjacent rows, leaving 4 threads between each set.

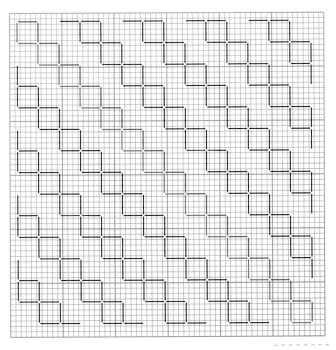

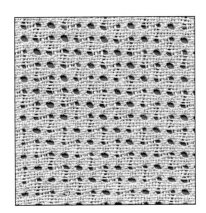

- Crossed-window fillings -

In this sample, I have left 1 thread in both directions between each row: this results in an attractive crossed-window filling. The effect of window fillings is less impressive if the wave stitch is too small: here I have worked it over 4 threads.

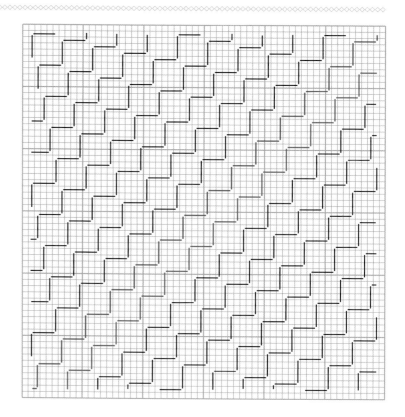

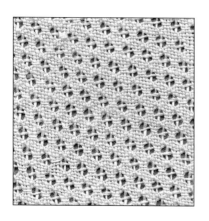

The combination of stitches creates a more complex pattern: here I have worked two adjacent rows, then left 1 vertical and 1 horizontal thread before working another two adjacent rows. The resulting effect is attractive alternating lines of windows and single-cross windows. The stitches were worked over 4 threads.

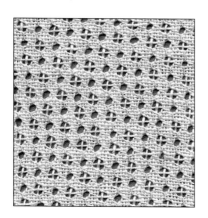

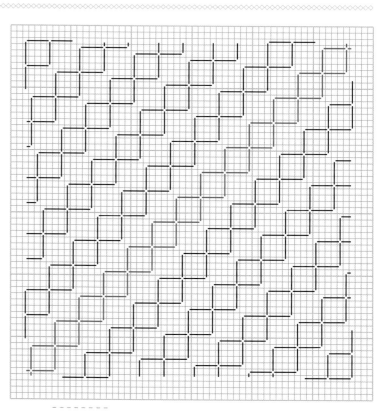

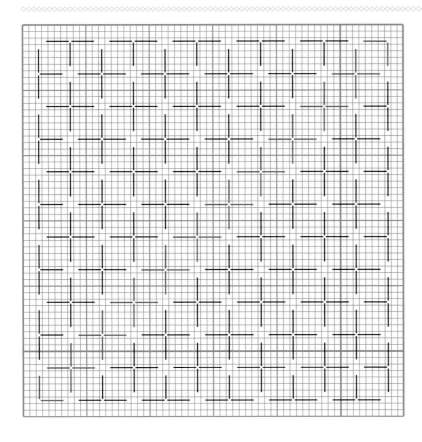

This filling is along the same lines as the previous one, resulting in lines of windows alternating with lines of double-cross windows. Only the basic line has changed: you embroider the groups of two stitches spaced 1 vertical and 1 horizontal thread apart. As with the previous filling, work two adjacent rows, leaving 1 thread before working the next set of two adjacent rows.

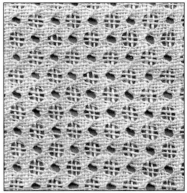

For sample 70, work as shown in the diagrams below. Start with the central row and work to one side first and then the other.

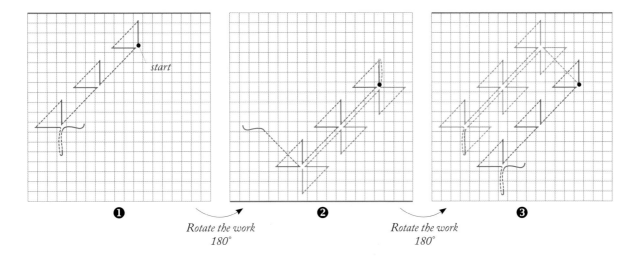

❶   Rotate the work
              180°

❷   Rotate the work
              180°

❸

You can obtain a filling of double-cross windows by slightly changing the basic line: you simply need to space all the stitches 1 vertical and 1 horizontal thread apart, and to space the rows in the same way as shown in the chart.

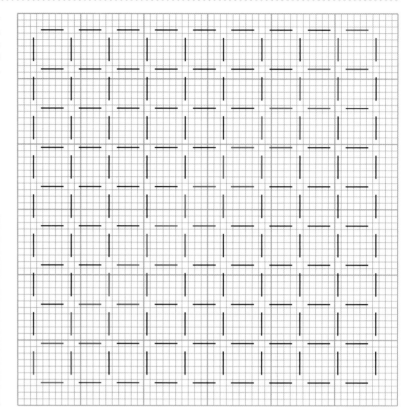

Start with the central row and work to one side first and then the other.

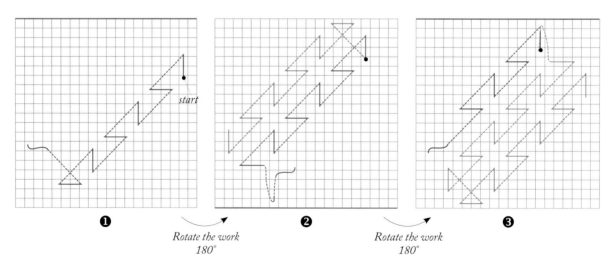

❶   *Rotate the work 180°*   ❷   *Rotate the work 180°*   ❸

- Widely spaced fillings -

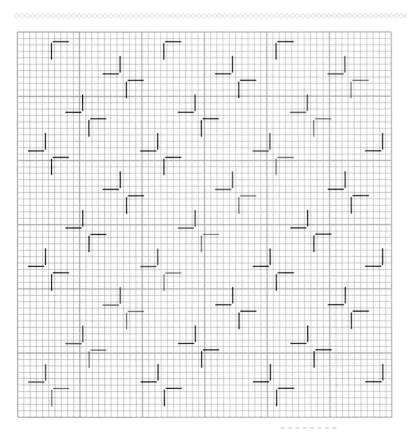

This filling is light and neat: the double rows of small windows in faggot stitch are easy to work, leaving 2 crosssed threads between each. It looks very elegant if you use a tiny stitch over 2 threads, as I have done here.

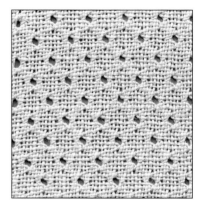

You can use the same technique to create widely spaced single-cross windows, spacing them as you choose.

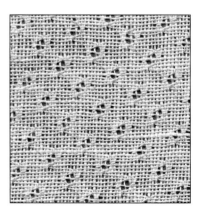

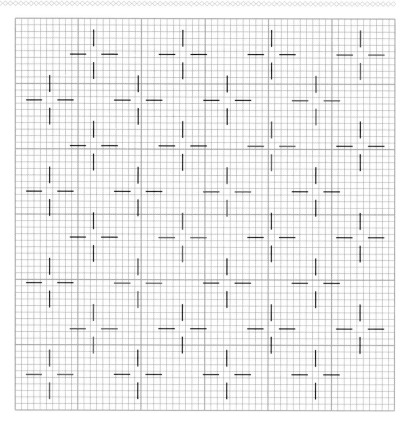

74 *worked using cordonnet no. 100*

This is another filling along the same lines, but resulting in double-cross windows. As in the previous samples, the effect is very light.

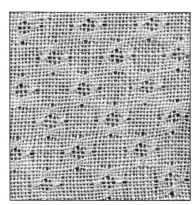

75 *worked using cordonnet no. 100*

Similar to the previous sample, this version is worked over 4 threads.

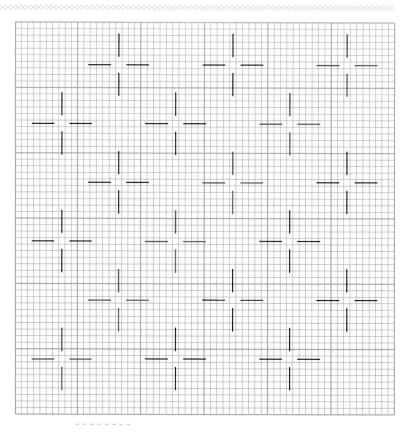

- Closely spaced fillings -

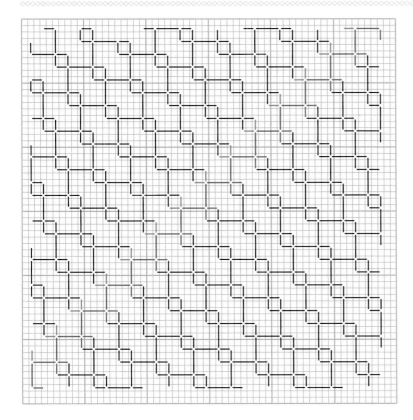

You can easily combine two sizes of stitches as shown here: one row of faggot stitch over 4 threads next to two rows of faggot stitch over 2 threads (see page 90).

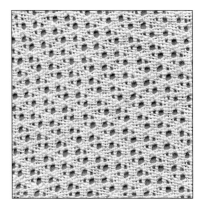

In this example, I have alternated two rows of faggot stitch over 4 threads and four rows of faggot stitch over 2 threads (see page 90). This pattern is the fruit of personal research: you can find others by experimenting with the same two basic variations.

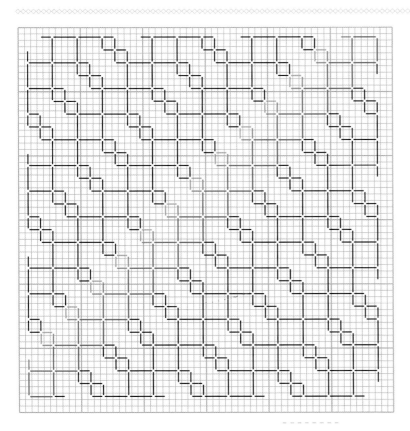

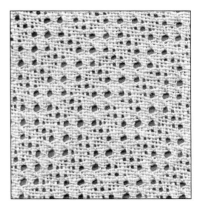

DOUBLE FAGGOT STITCH

Method

Double faggot stitch gives a bolder effect than the single version of the stitch because the threads of the fabric are pulled very tightly and the 'holes' are more defined. In its simplest form, it results in a small, very even grid, a pattern that appears to have been one of the most widespread and earliest examples of this technique. Its simplicity means it works well with traditional embroidery stitches or other openwork stitches, where each serves to highlight the other. As it wraps round a lot of the background thread, it can be used on less loosely woven fabrics than most other openwork stitches. It can be worked over 2, 3 or 4 threads, but it creates the best effect in more elaborate fillings if it is used over only a few threads, and in its simplest form for very small areas, which it suits to perfection.

It is worked **downwards from right to left**, using a fine thread, pulling hard to create the 'holes' in the fabric.

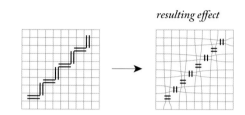

resulting effect

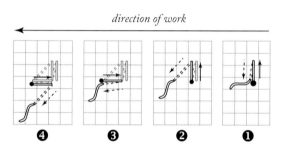

direction of work

❹   ❸   ❷   ❶

Fillings using double faggot stitch

worked using cordonnet no. 100

78

Two very simple fillings are shown here: single rows separated by 4 threads in the top left half, and rows worked side by side to give full coverage of the fabric in the bottom right half. The latter filling is the most widely used in modern times, and is perfect over small areas.

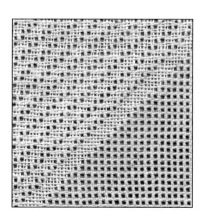

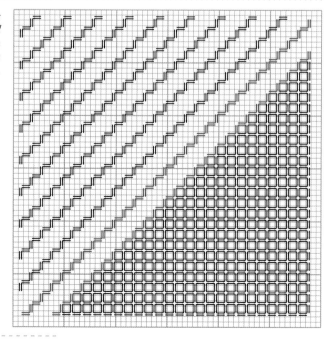

worked using cordonnet no. 100

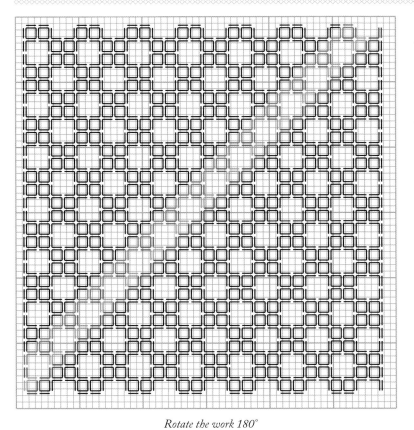

This is a very delicate openwork filling, obtained by leaving gaps on some of the rows. This technique can be used to obtain all sorts of patterns, by adjusting the spacing between stitches on the same row, which changes the ratio of the spaces left free between the worked stitches.

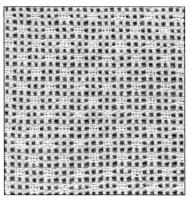

Rotate the work 180°

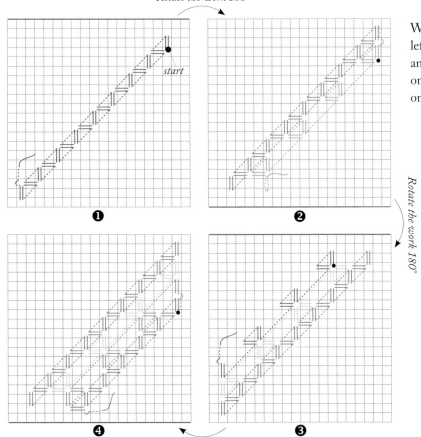

Work as shown in the diagrams, left. Start with the central row and then work all the rows on one side before starting the rows on the other side.

Rotate the work 180°

Rotate the work 180°

Rotate the work 180°

❶ start

❷

❸

❹

worked using cordonnet no. 100

This is similar to the previous filling (no. 79), but you combine the stitches differently. You can also experiment with working stitches over 3 threads instead of 2, depending on the fabric you are using and the effect you are trying to achieve (see design 81 below).

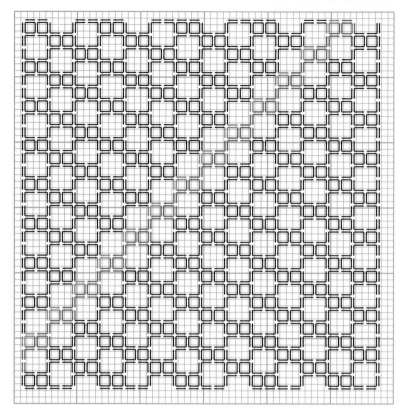

worked using cordonnet no. 100

This version was worked over 3 threads.

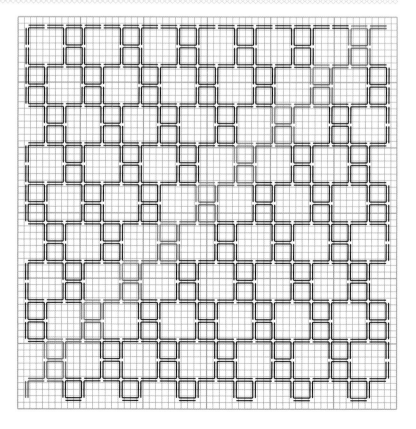

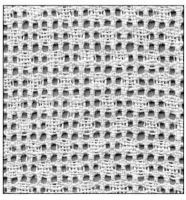

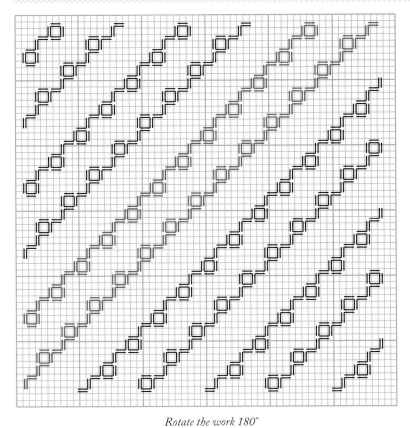

This light filling forms an attractive diagonal design. It is worked in a similar way to the previous example, but leaving 4 or 8 threads between the first two rows and the next two rows.

Start with the central row and first embroider just one side.

Rotate the work 180°

Rotate the work 180°

Rotate the work 180°

start

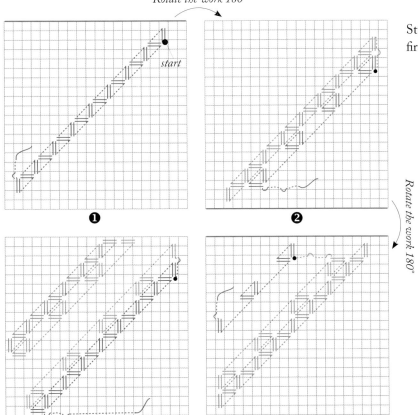

❶ ❷ ❸ ❹

Rotate the work 180°

You can obtain a huge variety of patterns in the same way. Here are a few charted designs to follow, but you can come up with your own ad infinitum.

 83 *worked using cordonnet no. 100*

Leaving gaps between sets of rows creates a strongly diagonal pattern.

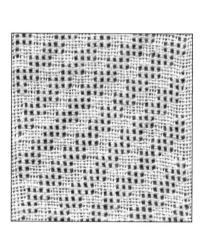

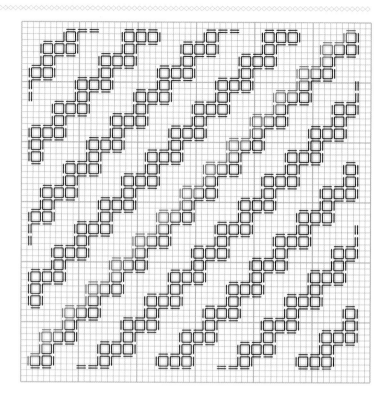

 84 *worked using cordonnet no. 100*

This variation is a lighter version of the previous one.

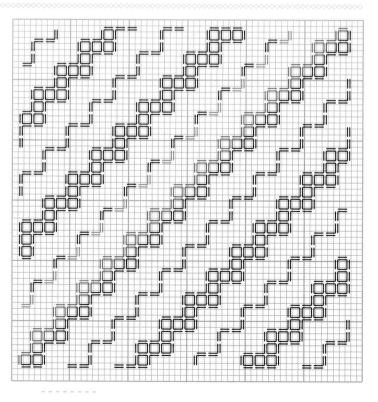

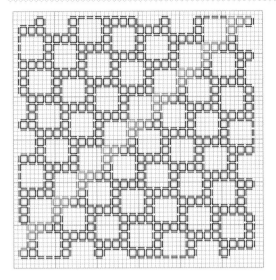

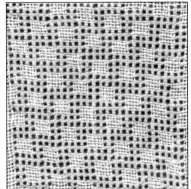

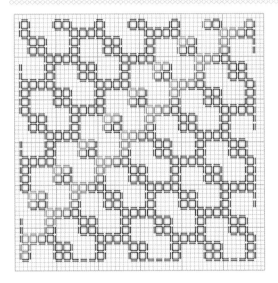

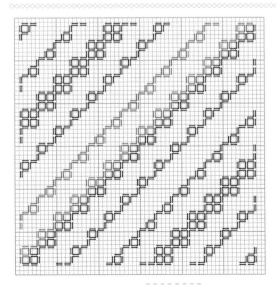

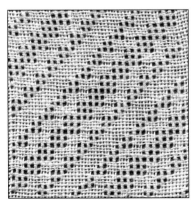

STAIRCASE STITCH

This is a variation of four-sided stitch in which you only need to work two sides, but you work each side twice. Work diagonally, as if creating a staircase.

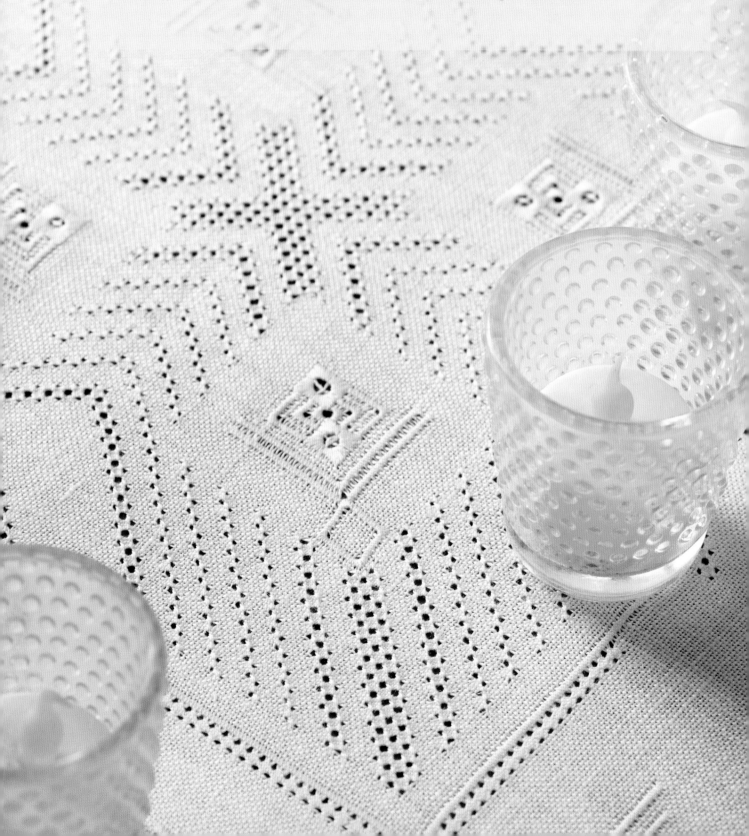

Method

- The basic stitch -

It is better to use a fine thread for this stitch to enhance the light result. Work from right to left upwards, pulling hard on the thread.

resulting effect

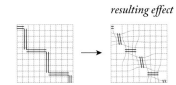

direction of work

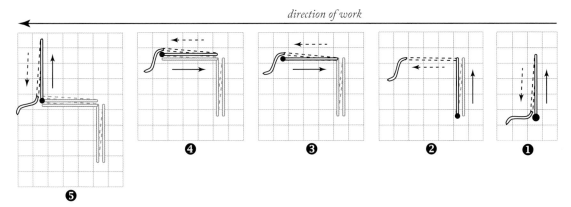

❺

To make the second row facing the first, you simply need to rotate your work 180° after the double horizontal stitch, and set off again in the normal fashion with a vertical stitch as shown in 2.

Rotate the work 180°

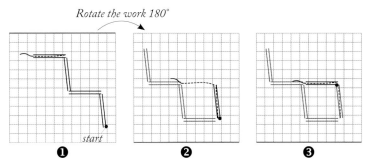

Try different combinations of single, double and triple lines for a wide variety of elegant patterns and fillings. This stitch works well with faggot stitch; they work well in composite designs together.

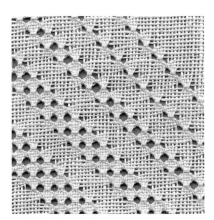

worked using cordonnet no. 100

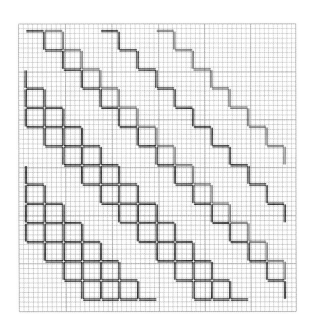

- Changing direction -

When you use staircase stitch as a line stitch, and you change direction, you must pay particular attention to the direction of the stitches. You have no doubt noticed that when you are working a single line, the stitches are not placed in the same way vertically as they are horizontally: the vertical stitches pull slightly to the diagonal while the horizontal stitches are very straight and tightly pulled. As a result, you must make sure that the stitches going in the same direction are all worked either horizontally or vertically (they can be worked symmetrically for the ones that are slightly diagonal).

Turning upwards (from your starting line):

After a double horizontal stitch, rotate 90° clockwise, and work downwards from left to right as follows:

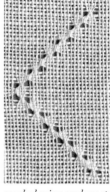

worked using cordonnet no. 100

Rotate the work 90° clockwise

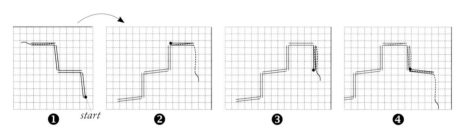

❶ *start* ❷ ❸ ❹

Turning downwards:

Rotate 90° anticlockwise, and work downwards from left to right as follows:

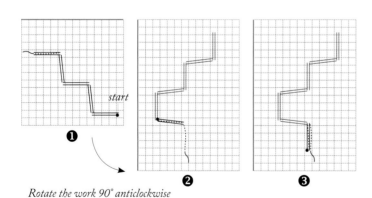

❶ *start* ❷ ❸

Rotate the work 90° anticlockwise

worked using cordonnet no. 100

Fillings using staircase stitch

Used on its own, staircase stitch forms light, diagonally oriented fillings. Play around with different combinations: single, double and triple lines, on their own or alternating. You can also create some attractive window fillings by leaving 1 or 2 threads between each row in both directions, or every other row.

Start with the central row and work to one side first and then the other.

- Simple staircase filling -

worked using dentelle no. 80

This is a simple, light filling that is a good choice when you need a fairly neutral design: I have simply left 4 threads between the rows, and embroidered the stitch itself over 4 threads.

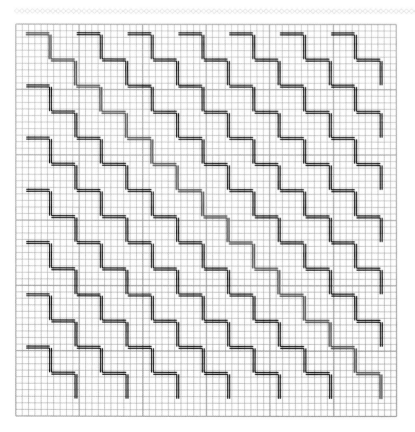

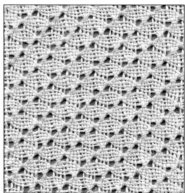

- Crossed-window fillings -

worked using dentelle no. 80

In this filling, the single rows are spaced 1 vertical and 1 horizontal thread apart: the windows appear across the whole area.

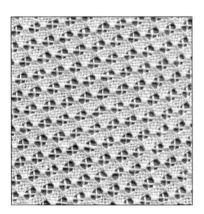

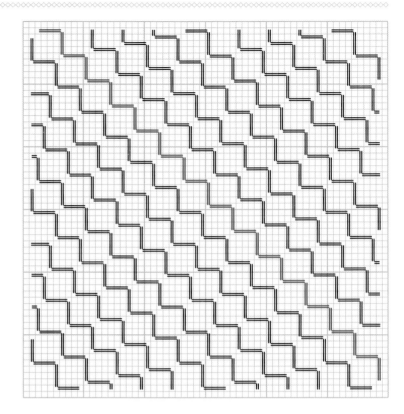

worked using cordonnet no. 100

In this filling, double rows are spaced 1 vertical and 1 horizontal thread apart: the uncrossed windows alternate with crossed windows, which makes the pattern a little more elaborate.

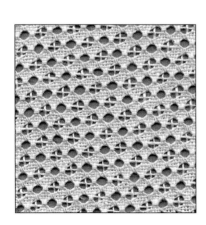

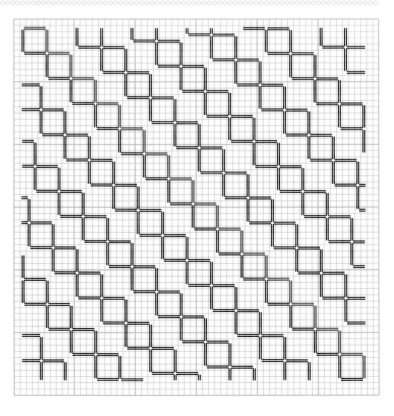

worked using dentelle no. 80

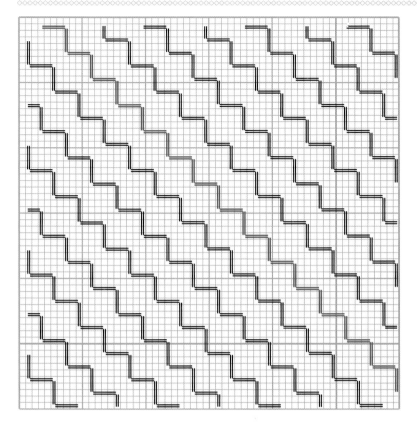

In this filling, I have spaced the rows 2 threads apart to obtain a light, double-cross window effect.

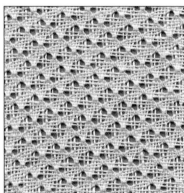

You could also try alternating uncrossed windows with double-cross windows, combining the ideas for samples 90 and 91. Experiment with the spacing between rows too, perhaps even alternating the spaces so that some rows are 2 threads apart and the others are 1 thread apart.

CROSS STITCH

UPRIGHT CROSS STITCH

Method

- - - - - - - - - - -

Whether you work in horizontal or diagonal lines, upright cross stitch forms a fairly solid, textured pattern line. It is most commonly used as a filling stitch, on its own or combined with others.

The stitch is worked over an even number of threads, usually 2 or 4. You will generally use a fairly round thread that is not too fine, in order to create interesting textures (coton à broder no. 20 or cordonnet no. 50 for example), but some fillings, especially crosses worked over 4 threads, are most effective with a finer thread. It is up to you to try the different options and see what you prefer.

- Working in horizontal lines -

In horizontal lines, the upright crosses should be worked one after the other, from right to left, pulling hard on the thread.

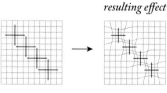

resulting effect

direction of work

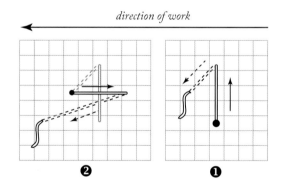

❷   ❶

- Working in diagonal lines -

When working in diagonal lines, first the vertical stitches are embroidered from right to left upwards, then the horizontal stitches are worked downwards, pulling hard on the thread in both cases.

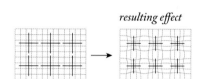

resulting effect

direction of work

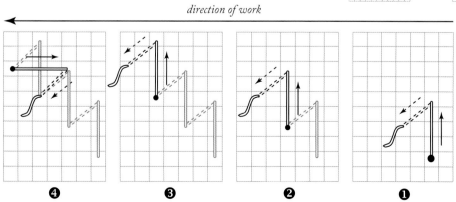

❹   ❸   ❷   ❶

Fillings using upright cross stitch

92 *worked using dentelle no. 80*

This simple filling is worked in horizontal lines, with each cross over 6 threads. The result is more attractive if you use fine thread, and it will form a lovely, light pattern.

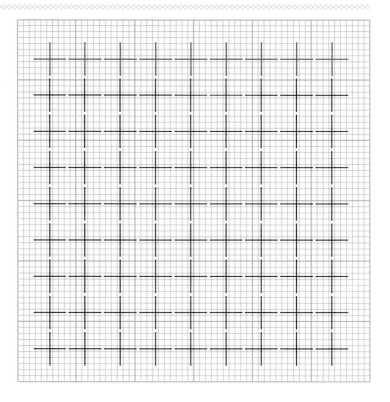

93 *worked using cordonnet no. 100*

This filling, like the following ones, is worked diagonally. Each cross is worked over 4 threads. Work the verticals first, from bottom left to top right, then come back down the line to add the horizontal stitches.

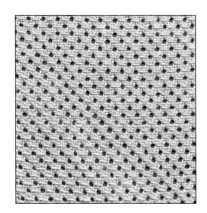

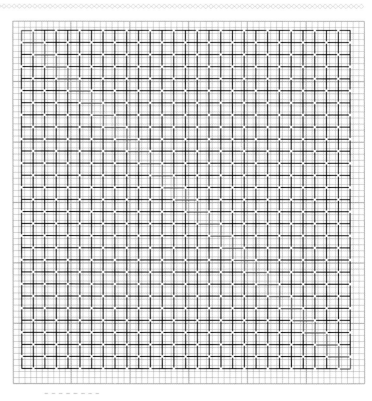

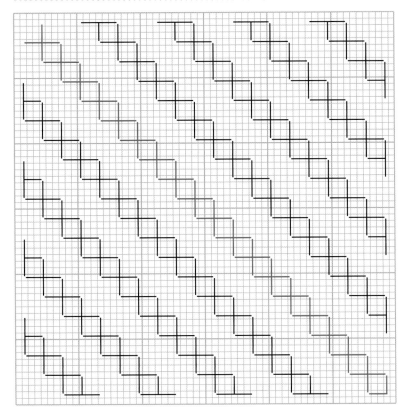

This time, leave 6 threads between each row to create a strongly diagonal filling. Each cross is worked over 6 threads here.

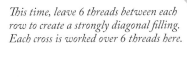

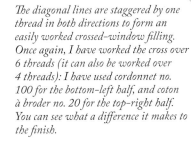

worked using cordonnet no. 100 and coton à broder no. 20

95

The diagonal lines are staggered by one thread in both directions to form an easily worked crossed-window filling. Once again, I have worked the cross over 6 threads (it can also be worked over 4 threads): I have used cordonnet no. 100 for the bottom-left half, and coton à broder no. 20 for the top-right half. You can see what a difference it makes to the finish.

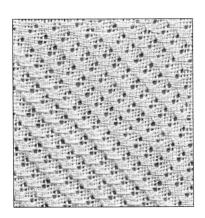

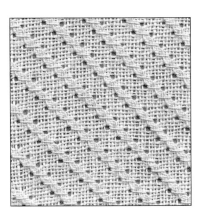

This grid is formed of two crossed layers of upright cross stitches over 4 threads. Each layer is formed of diagonal rows spaced 4 threads apart. A heavier thread gives the end result an attractive texture, which highlights the lighter, more open stitchwork.

You can also work it over 6 threads; it then forms a larger latticework that looks best when covering a larger area.

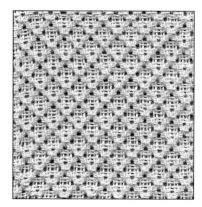

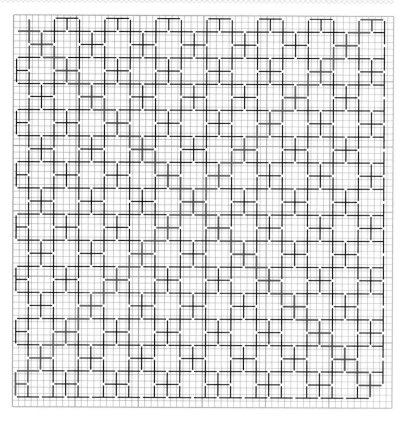

Start with the central row and work to one side first and then the other.

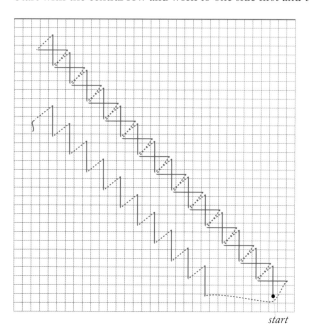

start

❶

Fill the required area with rows spaced at regular intervals. Start by working the vertical stitches of the row, then work back down with the horizontal ones.

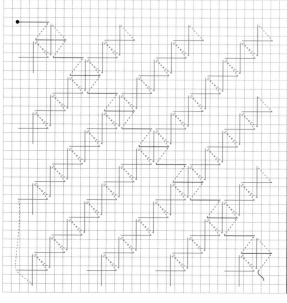

❷

Rotate the work 90° clockwise and then start again, crossing the rows: there will be two superimposed cross stitches at the point where they cross.
Note: to ensure that all your crosses are in the same direction, start with the horizontal stitch of the cross, therefore reversing the direction you are moving in.

PULLED CROSS STITCH

Method

- - - - - - - - - - -

Pulled cross stitch, worked so that it is pulled very tightly, forms a very open pattern. It is sometimes used as a filling stitch, either on its own or more often in combination with other stitches.

Use a fine thread, pulling hard to create the 'holes' in the fabric.

The stitch is worked in two parts; it can go from right to left, or from left to right, whichever you prefer, but always the same way, so that the stitch on top is always in the same direction. It can be worked singly or doubly, over an odd or even number of threads, depending on the effect you want to achieve: double gives greater texture and a more open effect, while single is lighter and for some patterns can be worked with a finer thread.

- Simple pulled cross stitch -

resulting effect

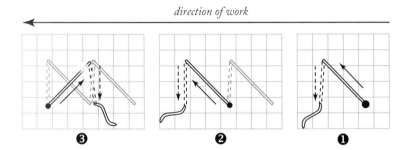

direction of work

❸   ❷   ❶

- Double pulled cross stitch -

resulting effect

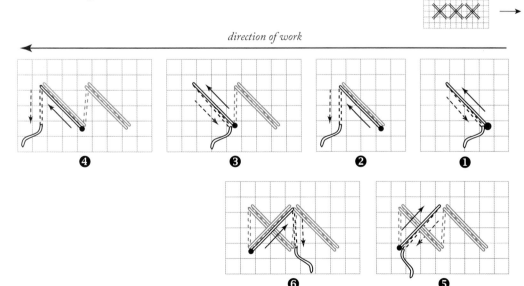

direction of work

❹   ❸   ❷   ❶

❻   ❺

- - - - - - - -

Fillings using pulled cross stitch

97 *worked using cordonnet no. 50*

Here is a very simple filling, which forms well-defined, horizontal bands. The example is worked over 4 threads.

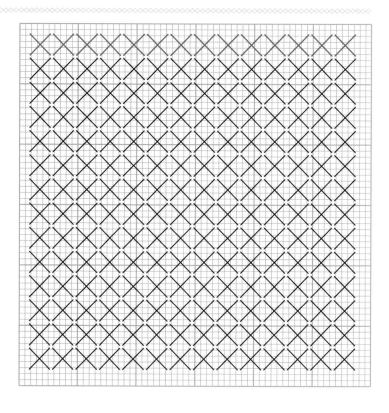

98 *worked using cordonnet no. 50*

This pattern is very similar to the previous one, but the stitches are staggered between rows: they must then be worked over an even number of threads. This example is worked over 4 threads.

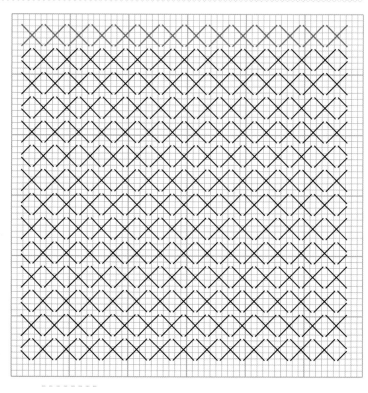

If this same pattern is worked using double crosses, the effect is notably different; as the stitches are pulled more tightly over the horizontal threads, the vertical threads of the fabric form a small zigzag between the rows. Here, I have worked over 4 threads.

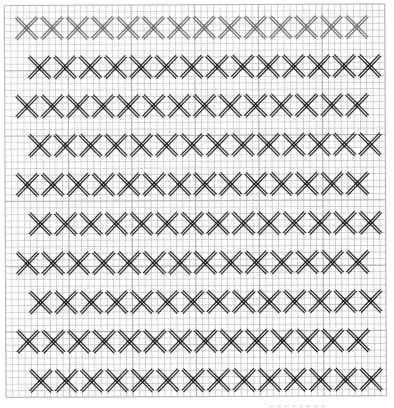

By leaving 1 or 2 threads between the rows, you achieve a new pattern, which has a straighter orientation.

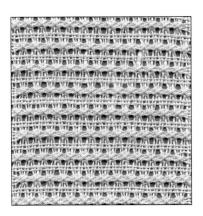

Still using double crosses, you can also leave 1 thread between each stitch and 1 thread between each row, this time working the rows facing each other and not staggered. This results in an attractive, very square, single-cross window filling. You can also try leaving 2 threads between each stitch and 2 threads between each row.

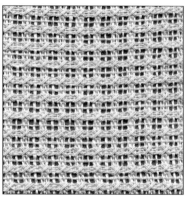

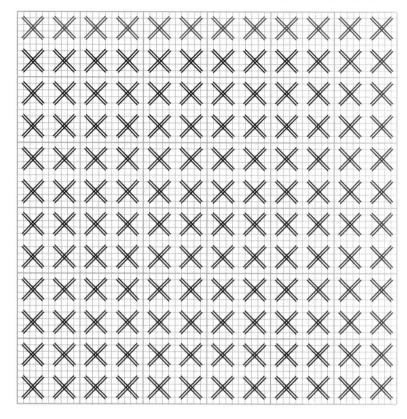

This is the same as the previous design but without leaving a thread between the rows or the stitches.

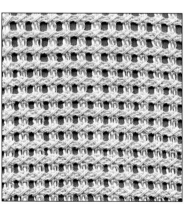

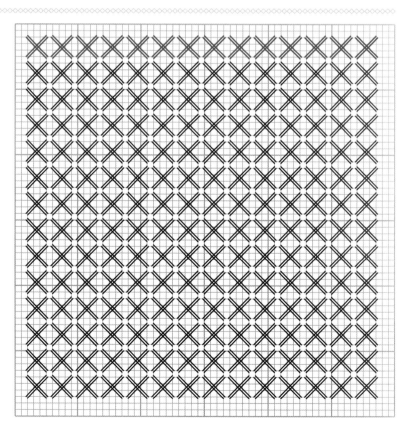

worked using cordonnet no. 100 (top) and coton à broder no. 30 (bottom) **103**

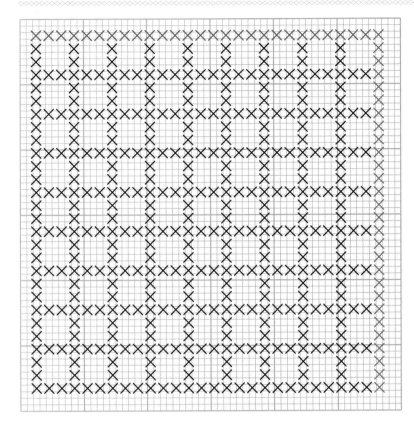

In this example, I have used the single cross stitch again, to create an elegant little grid pattern. The pattern is worked in two parts; the horizontal rows first, then the vertical rows, which are worked horizontally after having rotated the work 90°.

I have worked this sample over 2 threads, with 4 threads between each row.

worked using dentelle no. 80 **104**

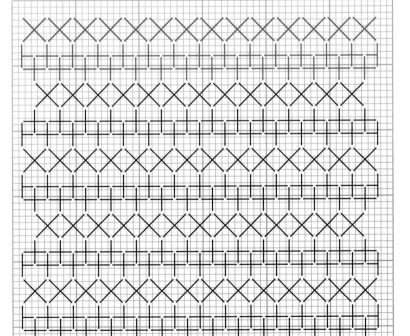

Here is an attractive composite filling, alternating rows of upright cross stitch with rows of pulled cross stitch. Work the whole area row by row.

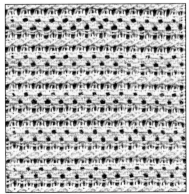

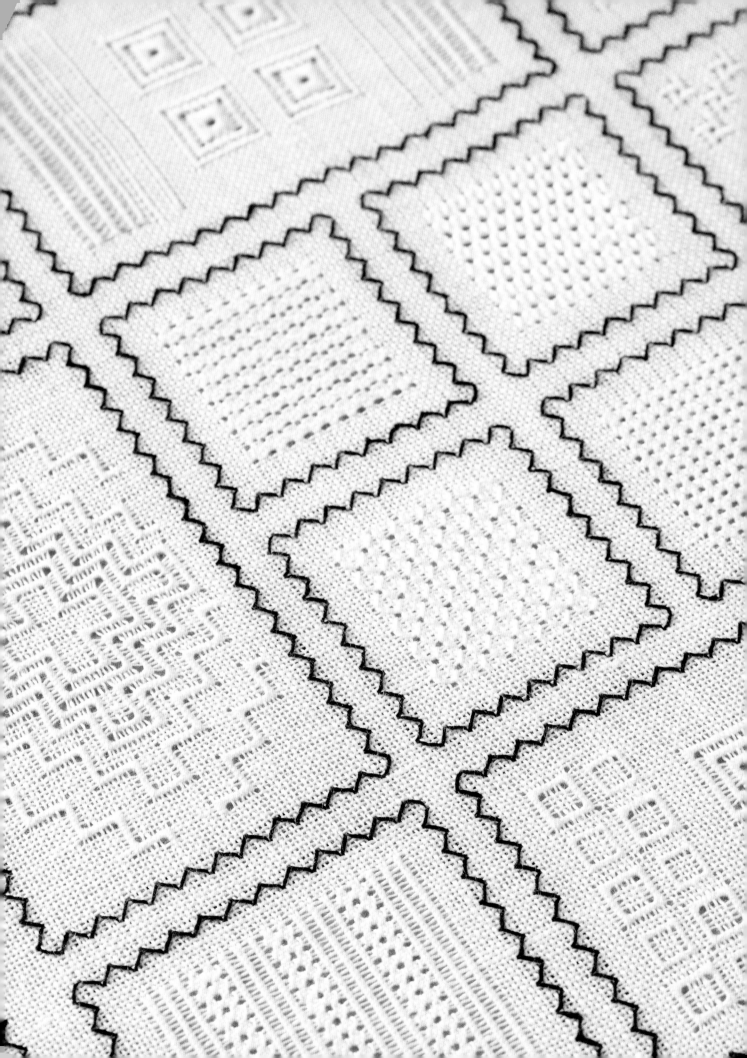

composite fillings

Until now, we have only looked at pulled thread fillings using each stitch on its own. Now we will look at patterns formed by combinations of stitches. Most of these are traditional designs used in some of the amazing embroidered pieces of the 18th century. Stitches can be combined in an infinite number of ways and you can give your imagination free rein in making up your own designs. As you have no doubt noticed, you often need do little more than change a single aspect of any given pattern to obtain a completely different end result; this might be stitch size, number of rows, number of threads between rows, and so on. Just give it a go and don't throw away any of your attempts; samples that seem of little interest in themselves may often come into their own on another project, and can sometimes be a springboard for new discoveries. Likewise, even mistakes can be interesting and lead you to discover something new. Correct them when you are in the middle of a particular embroidery project, but take a note of the result as you never know when they might come in useful.

Tip: when pulled satin stitch is used immediately adjacent to other stitches, you should ideally work it across the whole of the piece and then embroider any other pulled stitches subsequently, otherwise the satin stitch becomes more difficult to work.

105 *worked using dentelle no. 80 for the pulled satin stitch and stranded cotton for the satin stitch*

Stitches used:
• Straight pulled satin stitch
• Satin stitch

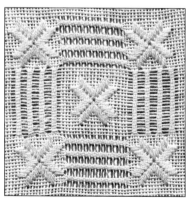

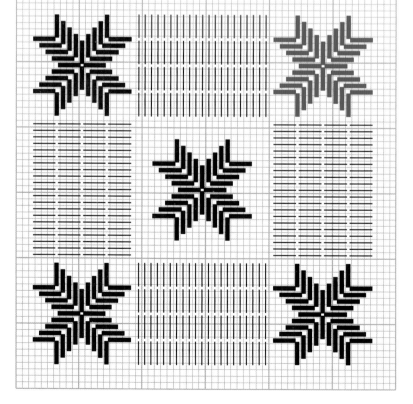

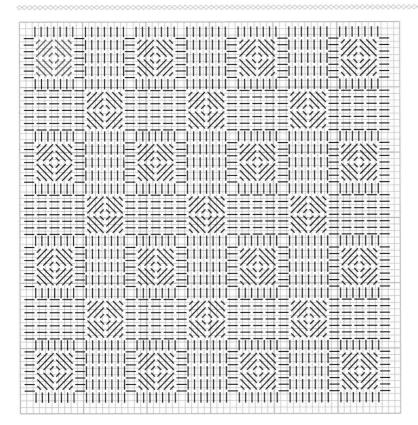

Stitches used:
- Straight pulled satin stitch
- Diagonal pulled satin stitch

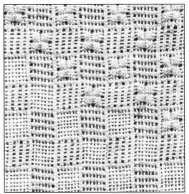

Stitches used:
- Straight pulled satin stitch
- Diagonal pulled satin stitch

Stitches used:
• Pulled satin stitch
• Four-sided stitch

First embroider the rows of pulled satin stitch in groups of three adjacent rows, leaving 8 threads between each group. Then work the two rows of four-sided stitch in the spaces in between.

Variation: *embroider the two rows of four-sided stitch in a brick pattern (see page 63).*

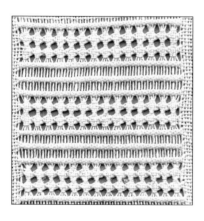

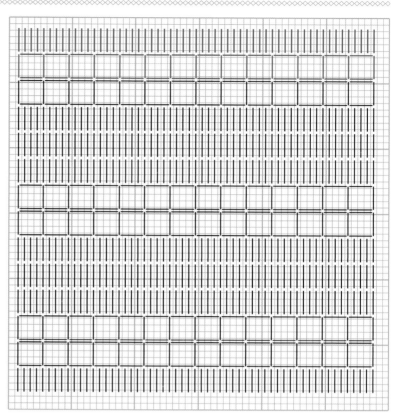

Stitches used:
• Pulled satin stitch
• Four-sided stitch in blocks

Embroider the three rows of pulled satin stitch one after the other, moving in steps from one block to the next. Then work the blocks of four-sided stitch.

Variation: *work blocks of four four-sided stitches and vary the length and number of rows of pulled satin stitch accordingly.*

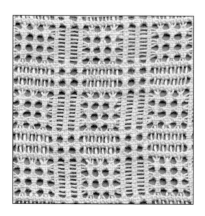

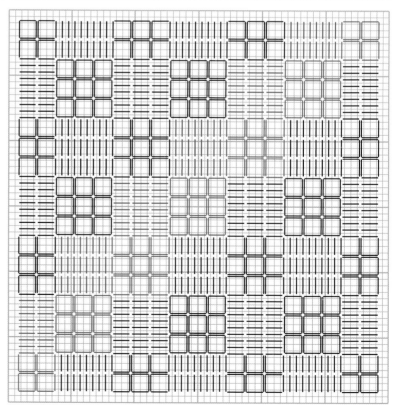

worked using cordonnet no. 100 **110**

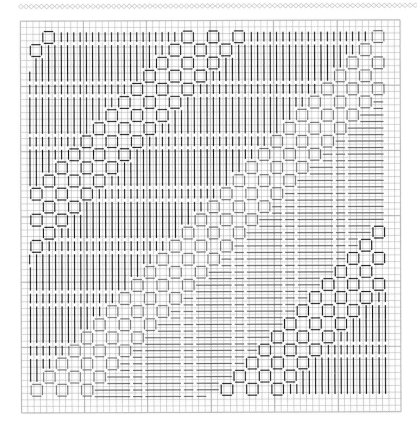

Stitches used:
• Pulled satin stitch
• Diagonal four-sided stitch

Start by embroidering the centre of the pattern with the rows of diagonal four-sided stitch. Then embroider the rows of pulled satin stitch, then the four-sided stitch, and so on. Pay attention to the direction the rows of pulled satin stitch are going in.

Variation: *embroider all the pulled satin stitches in the same direction.*

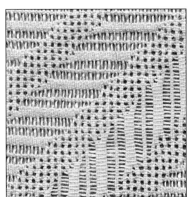

worked using cordonnet no. 100 **111**

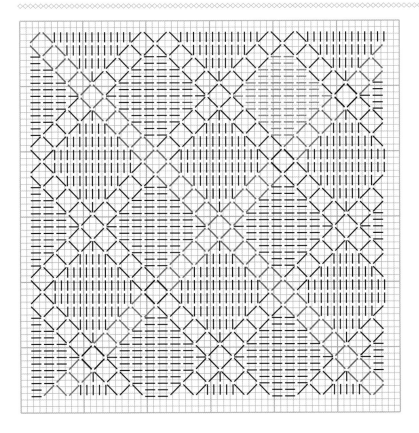

Stitches used:
• Pulled satin stitch
• Diagonal four-sided stitch

Start by embroidering the grid of diagonal four-sided stitch, starting with the row in the middle. Then work the pulled satin stitch in the spaces defined by the previous rows: pay attention to the direction the rows are going in.

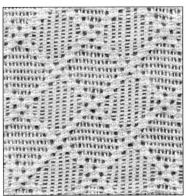

Stitches used:
• Pulled satin stitch
• Diagonal four-sided stitch

Start by embroidering the central row of diagonal four-sided stitch, then embroider the rows of pulled satin stitch, then the four-sided stitch, and so on.

Pay attention to the direction that the rows of pulled satin stitch are going in.

Variation: *work all the rows of pulled satin stitch horizontally – the effect can be interesting in some patterns.*

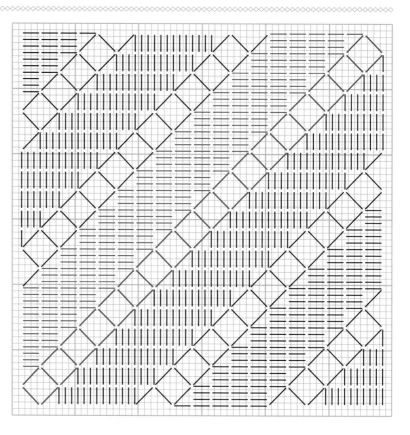

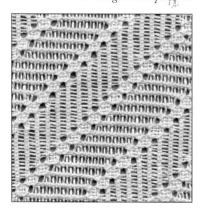

Stitches used:
• Diagonal satin stitch (unpulled)
• Diagonal four-sided stitch

First embroider the grid of four-sided stitch, starting with the central row: there will be 2 four-sided stitches on top of each other at the point where the rows cross. Then work the small blocks of satin stitch.

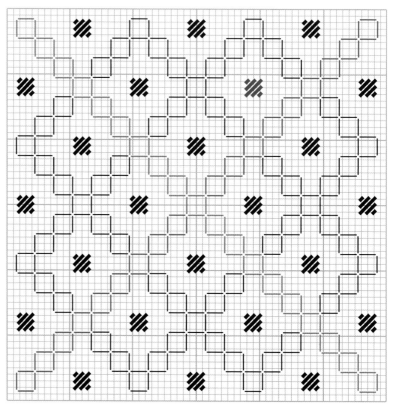

worked with coton à broder no. 25

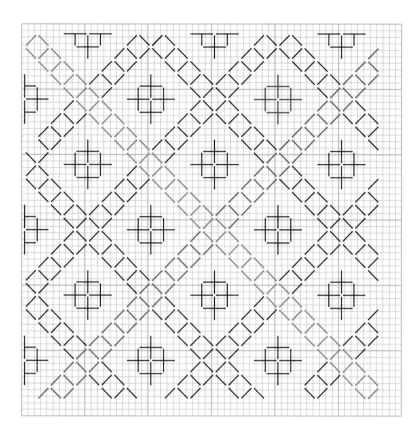

Stitches used:
- Upright cross stitch
- Diagonal four-sided stitch

Work the central row diagonally, then the parallel rows on either side of it, referring to the chart. Start again on the opposite diagonal (there will be 2 superimposed four-sided stitches at the point where the rows intersect). Finally, work the blocks of upright crosses.

worked with coton à broder no. 20

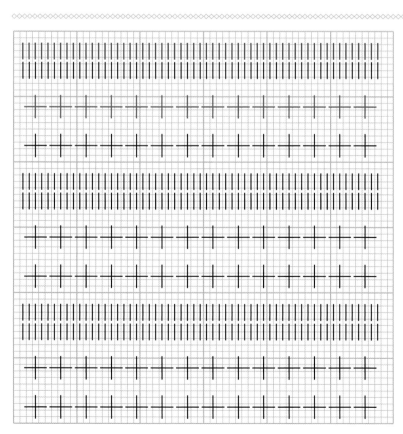

Stitches used:
- Pulled satin stitch
- Upright cross stitch

Work two rows of pulled satin stitch over 3 threads, leave 2 threads, work one row of upright crosses, leave 2 threads, work one row of upright crosses, leave 2 threads, and so on.

Variations: *work the two rows of upright crosses closer together, or interlock them. You could also experiment with a finer thread.*

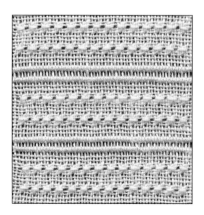

Stitches used:
- Pulled satin stitch
- Upright cross stitch

Embroider the rows of upright crosses and pulled satin stitch in the order shown in the chart.

Variation: *leave one thread between the rows of pulled satin stitch.*

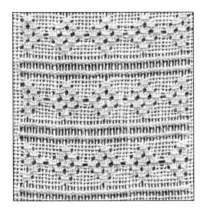

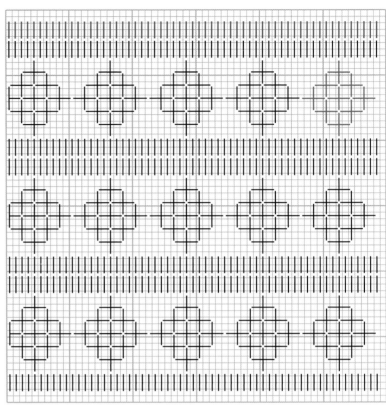

Stitches used:
- Pulled satin stitch
- Upright cross stitch

Embroider the vertical rows of upright crosses and the blocks of pulled satin stitch and upright crosses in turn, following the chart.

Variation: *replace the upright crosses with another stitch, for example four-sided stitch.*

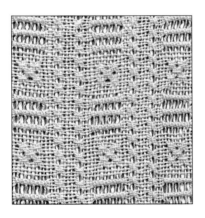

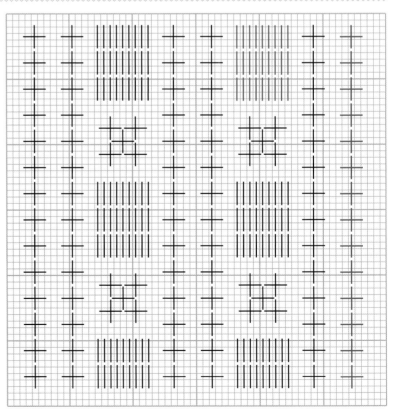

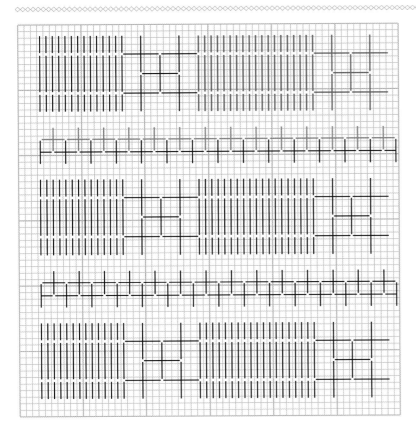

Stitches used:
• Pulled satin stitch
• Upright cross stitch

Embroider the horizontal rows of upright crosses and the blocks of pulled satin stitch and upright crosses in turn, following the chart.

Variation: *replace the double row of upright crosses with a triple row of reverse wave stitches over 2 threads vertically.*

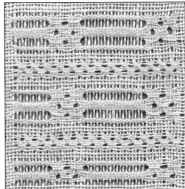

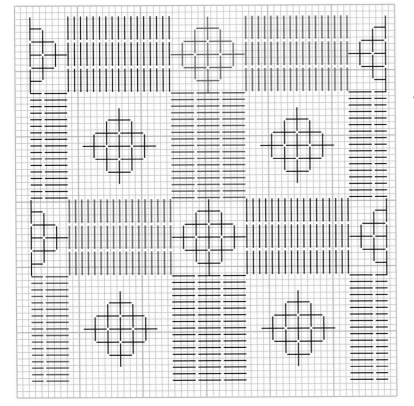

Stitches used:
• Pulled satin stitch
• Upright cross stitch

Embroider the three rows of pulled satin stitch one after the other, moving in steps from one block to the next. Then work the upright cross blocks between the pulled satin stitch blocks.

Variation: *replace the three rows of pulled satin stitch over 4 threads, with four rows over 3 threads.*

Stitches used:
• Pulled satin stitch
• Upright cross stitch

Embroider the three rows of pulled satin stitch one after the other, moving in steps from one block to the next. Then work the blocks of upright cross stitch.

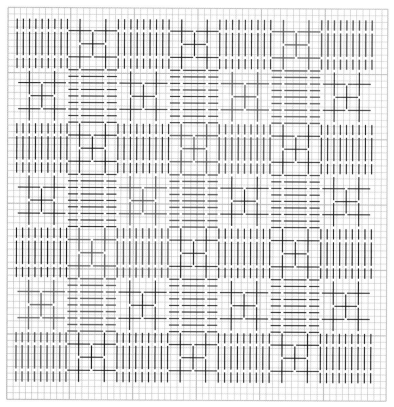

Stitches used:
• Pulled satin stitch
• Upright cross stitch

First embroider the grid of upright crosses, then the blocks of pulled satin stitch inside them.

Variations: *replace the three rows of pulled satin stitch over 4 threads, with four rows over 3 threads, or work the central row over 6 threads and the two outside rows over 2 threads.*

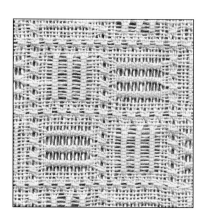

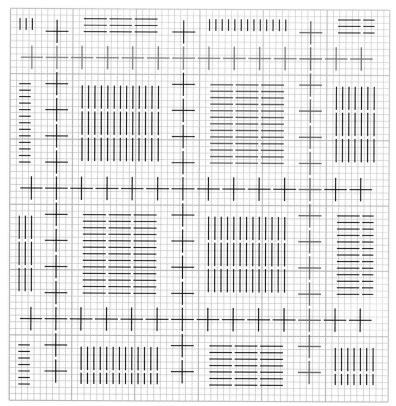

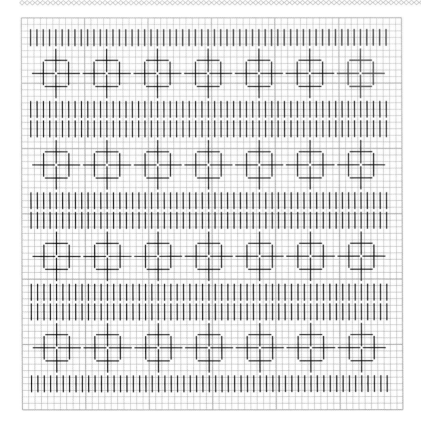

Stitches used:
• Pulled satin stitch
• Upright cross stitch

Embroider the rows of upright crosses and pulled satin stitch in the order shown in the chart.

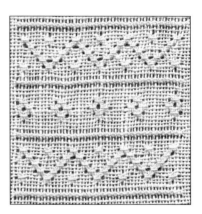

Stitches used:
• Pulled satin stitch
• Upright cross stitch

Embroider the rows of pulled satin stitch, then the rows of upright cross stitch in the order shown in the chart.

Variation: *leave 1 thread between the rows of pulled satin stitch.*

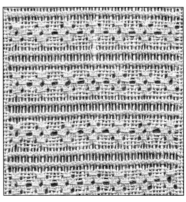

124

Stitches used:
- Pulled satin stitch
- Upright cross stitch

Embroider the pulled satin stitch patterns and rows of upright crosses alternately.

Variation: *instead of separating the row of pulled satin stitch into three rows over 2 threads, separate it into two rows over 3 threads.*

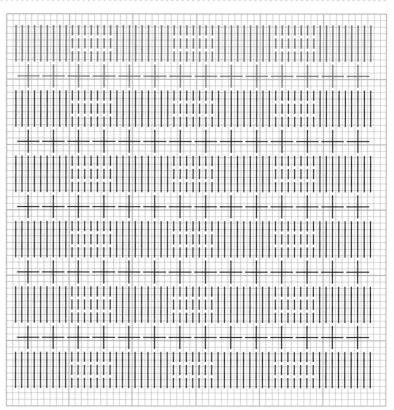

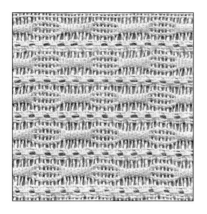

125

Stitches used:
- Satin stitch (unpulled)
- Upright cross stitch

Embroider the rows of satin stitches and upright crosses alternately, leaving 5 threads between each row.

Variations: *you can replace the upright crosses with one double row of diagonal wave stitch over 2 threads.*

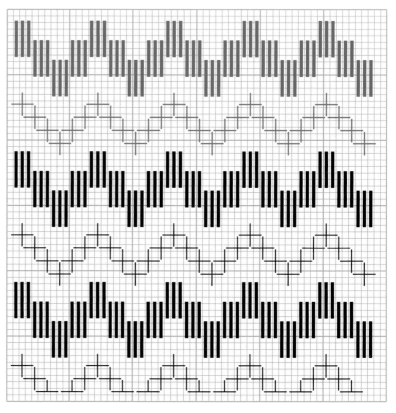

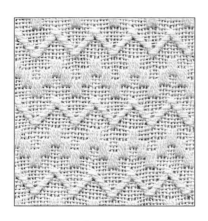

worked with coton à broder no. 30 and two strands of stranded cotton for the satin stitch

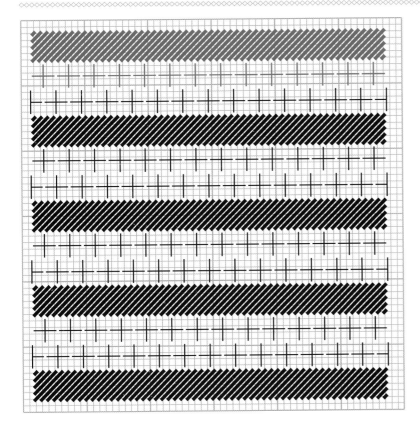

Stitches used:
- Diagonal satin stitch
- Upright cross stitch

Start by embroidering the rows of (unpulled) diagonal satin stitches, separated by 8 threads, then work two rows of upright crosses in the spaces.

Variation: *embroider three rows of closer intersecting upright crosses instead of two.*

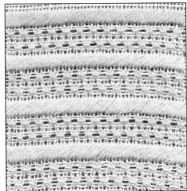

worked with cordonnet no. 50 and three strands of stranded cotton for the satin stitch

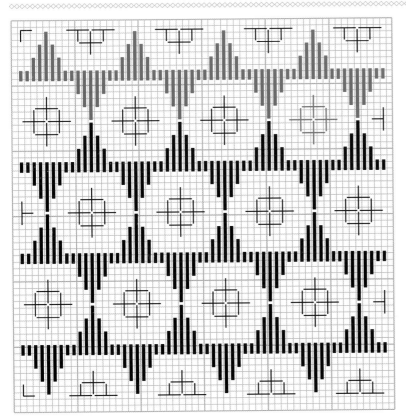

Stitches used:
- Satin stitch
- Upright cross stitch

Start by embroidering the (unpulled) satin stitch, following the diagram, then the upright crosses in the spaces that it has defined.

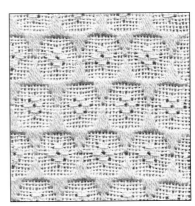

worked with coton à broder no. 30 and three strands of stranded cotton for the satin stitch

Stitches used:
• Satin stitch
• Upright cross stitch

Start by embroidering the rows of (unpulled) satin stitches, following the chart, then the upright crosses in the spaces in between.

Variations: *you can change the spacing and dimensions of the satin stitch rows.*

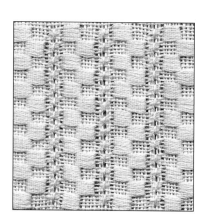

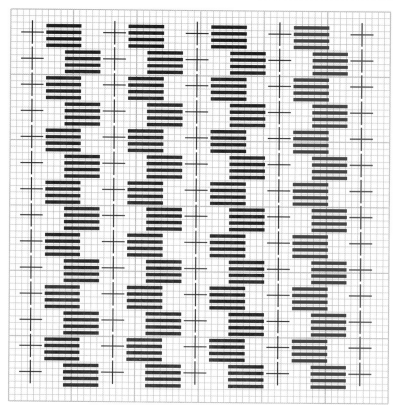

worked with cordonnet no. 100 and three strands of stranded cotton for the satin stitch

Stitches used:
• Satin stitch
• Upright cross stitch

Start by embroidering the rows of (unpulled) satin stitch, following the chart, then the upright crosses in the spaces between the double rows.

Variations: *replace the crosses with a double row of faggot stitch.*

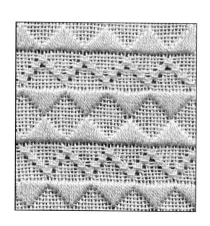

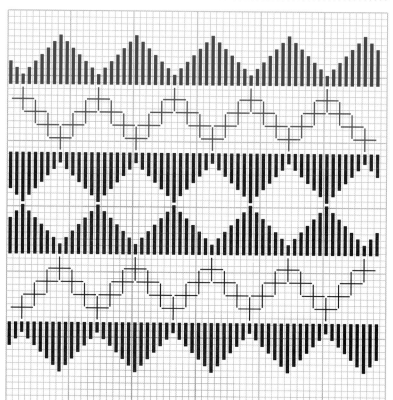

worked with cordonnet no. 100 and three strands of stranded cotton for the satin stitch **130**

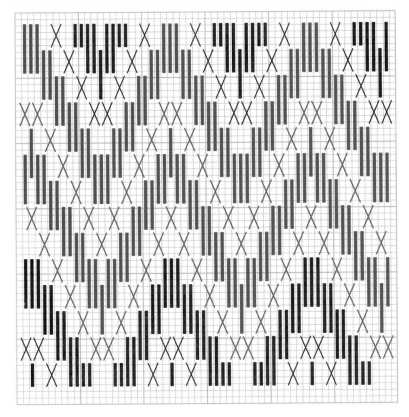

Stitches used:
• Satin stitch
• Cross stitch

Start by embroidering the rows of (unpulled) satin stitch, following the chart, then work the crosses (over 4 threads vertically and 2 horizontally) in the spaces between the satin stitch rows.

worked with coton à broder no. 25 **131**

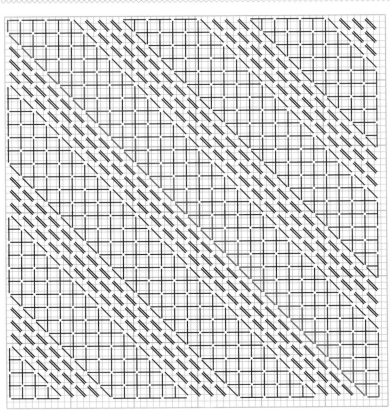

Stitches used:
• Upright cross stitch
• Reverse faggot stitch

Work the central row of upright cross stitches on the diagonal over 4 threads then two other adjacent rows. Then embroider four rows of reverse faggot stitch over 2 threads. Alternate these two series of stitches.

Variation: *change the number of rows of each stitch.*

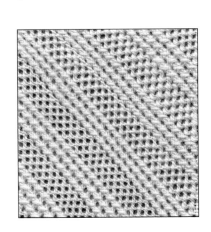

Stitches used:
• Faggot stitch
• Upright cross stitch

Embroider alternately three rows of faggot stitch and one diagonal row of upright crosses, using the same thread.

Variation: *change the number of rows in one or both of the stitches or the spacing of the rows.*

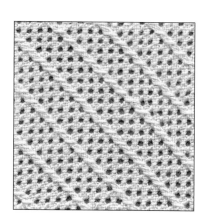

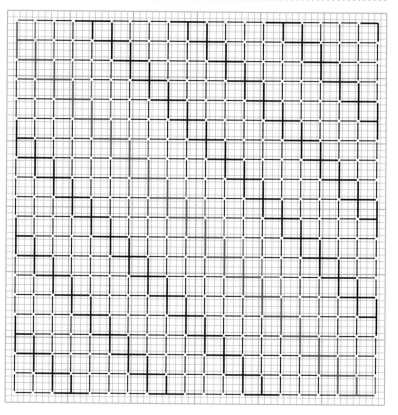

Stitches used:
• Reverse faggot stitch
• Faggot stitch

First embroider the double rows of reverse faggot stitch over 2 threads, leaving 12 threads between each. Then work the eyelet effect using faggot stitch in the spaces between them.

Variations: *replace the reverse faggot stitch with diagonal satin stitch or one diagonal row of upright crosses.*

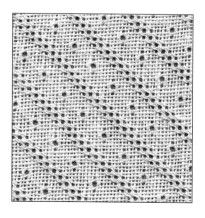

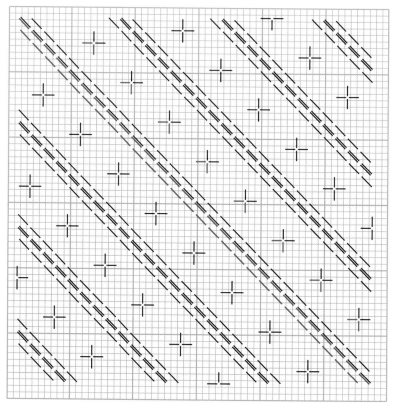

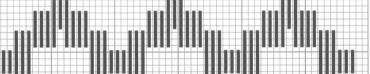

Stitches used:
• Faggot stitch
• Reverse faggot stitch

Embroider alternately one row of faggot stitch and one row of reverse faggot stitch to cover the required area.

Variation: *try changing the number of rows: two rows of each stitch, for example.*

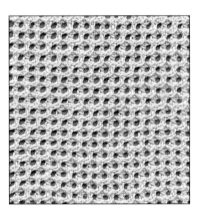

Stitches used:
• Satin stitch
• Reverse faggot stitch

Embroider alternately the satin stitch pattern and the zigzag using reverse faggot stitch, leaving 5 threads between the two and changing thread.

Variation: *embroider two rows of small cross stitches over 2 threads in the spaces inside the satin stitch patterns.*

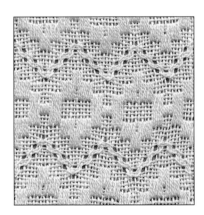

Stitches used:
• Satin stitch
• Reverse faggot stitch

*Start by embroidering the double rows of
reverse faggot stitch, following the chart;
then work in the opposite direction to
create a grid. Then work the satin stitch
patterns in the spaces created, following
the chart.*

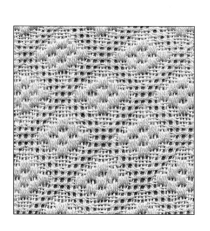

Stitches used:
• Pulled satin stitch
• Reverse wave stitch

*Start by working one row of pulled satin
stitch, with just one stitch every 2 threads.
Leave 2 threads.
Then embroider two rows of reverse wave
stitch over 4 threads horizontally and
4 threads vertically. Leave 2 threads.
Alternate these two series of stitches.*

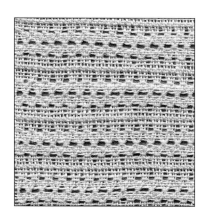

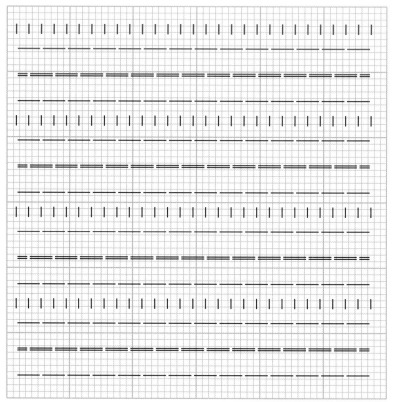

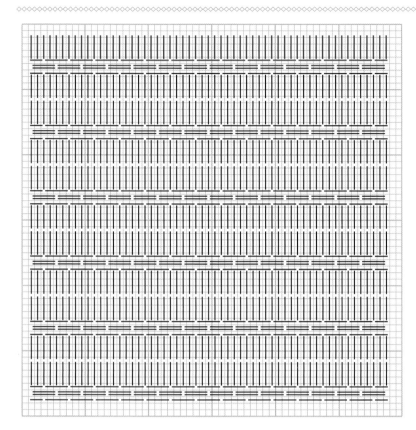

Stitches used:
- Pulled satin stitch
- Cable stitch (see page 78)

Embroider the rows of pulled satin stitch so that you open large holes between the two rows (by pulling the thread flat along your fabric in the opposite direction to your second row). Leave 2 threads between each double row worked in this way. Work cable stitch over these 2 threads.

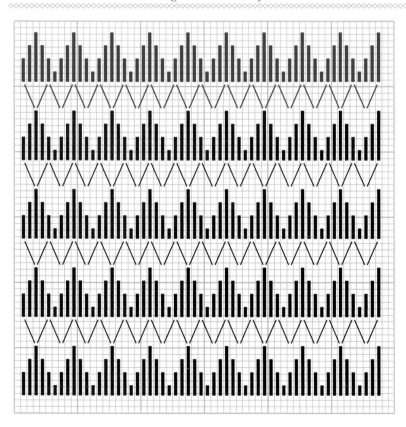

Stitches used:
- Satin stitch
- Wave stitch

Start by embroidering the satin stitch triangles, leaving 4 threads between the rows. Then work wave stitch over 4 threads vertically and 2 threads horizontally in the spaces formed.

Stitches used:
- Pulled satin stitch
- Wave stitch

First embroider the double rows of pulled satin stitch over 3 threads, leaving 8 threads between each. Then create small windows using wave stitch over 2 threads spaced 4 threads apart in the spaces.

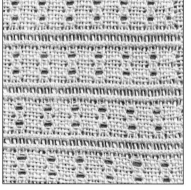

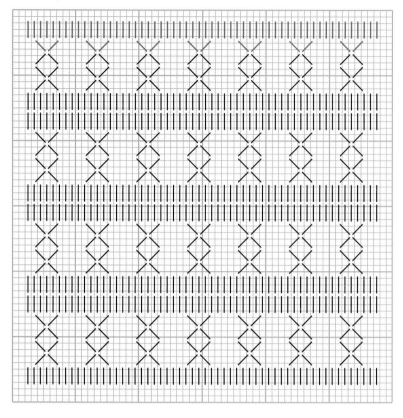

worked using cordonnet no. 100

Stitches used:
- Pulled satin stitch
- Double faggot stitch

Start by working the double faggot stitch following the chart, then work the rows of pulled satin stitch in the spaces.

Variations: *double faggot stitch lends itself to numerous variations: discover them at your leisure.*

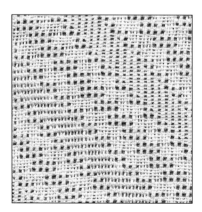

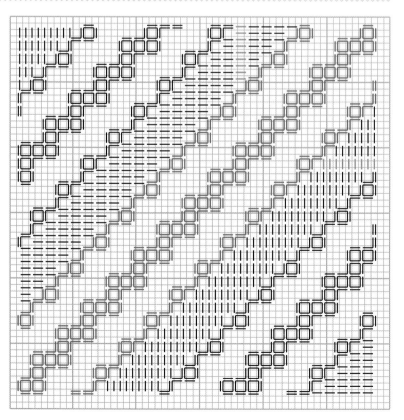

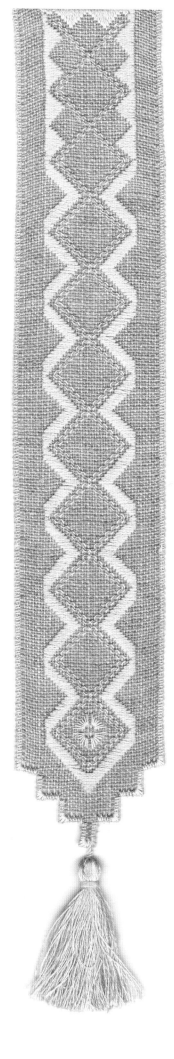

Index of fillings

Here are the filling numbers listed by stitch used:

Pulled satin stitch

1 to 45

composite fillings:
105, 106, 107, 108, 109, 110, 111, 112, 115, 116, 117, 118, 119, 120, 121, 122, 123, 124, 137, 138, 140, 141

Satin stitch (unpulled)

not numbered page 53

composite fillings:
105, 113, 125, 126, 127, 128, 129, 130, 135, 136, 139

Four-sided stitch

46 to 54

composite fillings:
108, 109, 110, 111, 112, 113, 114

Reverse wave stitch

55, 56, 57, 58 (cable stitch)

composite fillings:
137, 138 (cable stitch)

Reverse faggot stitch

59–61

composite fillings:
131, 133, 134, 135, 136

Wave stitch

62–65

composite fillings:
132, 133, 134, 139, 140

Faggot stitch

66–77

composite fillings:
132, 133, 134

Double faggot stitch

78–87

composite fillings:
141

Upright cross stitch

92–96

composite fillings:
114, 115, 116, 117, 118, 119, 120, 121, 122, 123, 124, 125, 126, 127, 128, 129, 131, 132

Staircase stitch

88–91

Pulled cross stitch

97–104

composite fillings:
130

Marie-Hélène Jeanneau
1951-2018

'I can't say how or when my love for embroidery was sparked, but it no doubt has something to do with my admiration for an aunt who was a remarkable embroiderer. She had an amazing talent for infinitely delicate creations, and this benchmark, along with the influence of an uncle who was an artist, has always made me see embroidery as drawing created with different tools.'

Marie-Hélène Jeanneau was a native of Cholet, a region with a strong linen tradition, and learnt to embroider as a young child, as was the norm. In a family environment of nature lovers, experts and observers her first passion was for geology and botany, disciplines that she would continue to explore throughout her life.

It was in the 1970s, a time of creative expansion, that she developed her interest in the textile arts. Personal experimentation led her to discover a vast field of expression and creativity in which the needle was the tool for creating colour, light, texture and design.

'As I explored the textile world, I worked more and more with embroidery, which attracted me far beyond its traditional usage, for its infinite possibilities in terms of the interplay of design, textures and materials that it allows.'

In the course of this journey of discovery, Marie-Hélène came across pulled thread work – a perfect alliance of creativity and geometric rigour, and began to explore this technique from a contemporary angle.

By the late 1980s embroidery had became a full-time pursuit. She then began to create her own collections and design exclusive models for a professional client base: embroidered buttons – a speciality of hers, children's accessories and household linen. The majority of her fresh and sophisticated designs are based on inspiration from the natural world and historic embroidery. She also organized and ran embroidery workshops.

In 1992, Marie-Hélène started her ten-year career as a writer. However, she never stopped embroidering and took it up again professionally in 2008 after training in other techniques led her to discover other areas of the embroidery world (Luneville crochet embroidery techniques and the restoration of old embroidery and furnishings). She then began to design pulled thread embroidery patterns for enthusiasts of embroidery, patchwork and other creative arts to stitch themselves, as well as offering courses and internships in embroidery with a strongly creative approach.

In her quest to explore the interplay of colours and materials Marie-Hélène developed a preference for natural fabrics (silk, linen, and so on), as well as for graphic designs growing from the stitches themselves. By seeking inspiration from multiple sources, she sought to give ancient techniques a modern twist, creating new designs to embellish everyday objects.

Marie-Hélène had a passion for sharing this taste for discovery and creation: *'I believe that we all have creative abilities deep within ourselves, and it is essential to awaken them, while at the same time providing the technical tools to do so.'*

Bibliography

Encyclopaedia of Needlework, Th. de Dillmont,
D.M.C. library, 1980

Danish Pulled Thread Embroidery, Esther Fangel,
Ida Winckler & Agnete Wuldem Madsen,
Dover Publications, Inc. New York, 1977

Drawn Fabric Embroidery, Agnes M. Leach,
Dover Publications, Inc. New York, 2001

Drawn Fabric Embroidery, Edna Wark,
B. T. Batsford, 1979

Pulled Thread Embroidery, Moyra McNeill,
Mills & Boon, London, 1971

Sources

Victoria & Albert Museum, London, UK
www.vam.ac.uk

Museum of Fine Arts, Boston, USA
www.mfa.org

Design Museum Denmark
www.designmuseum.dk

Museum of Rurual Life and the Headdress, Souvigné,
France
www.musee-souvigne.com and other rural museums
across the world where you can find headdresses and
garments embroidered using these techniques.

Thanks to

Jacques and my children;

Agnès, Claire-Lise, Mico;

Everyone who supported me in my research and
showed a close interest in my work;

My Aunt Marcelle, an exceptionally talented
embroiderer, who was my point of reference
throughout my journey in embroidery;

Alexis Faja, who understood my work and had
confidence in me from the start;

Éditions Burda for their publications, which led me
to discover this astonishingly rich technique.